TheoPsych

A Psychological Science Primer for Theologians

ISBN (paperback): 979-8-9858520-0-4
ISBN (ebook): 979-8-9858520-1-1

Cover design and formatting by Albatross Book Co.
albatrossbookco.com

Lightbulb illustration by Sierra Barrett

For permission requests, please contact: connect@blueprint1543.org

TheoPsych

A Psychological Science Primer *for* Theologians

Justin L. Barrett

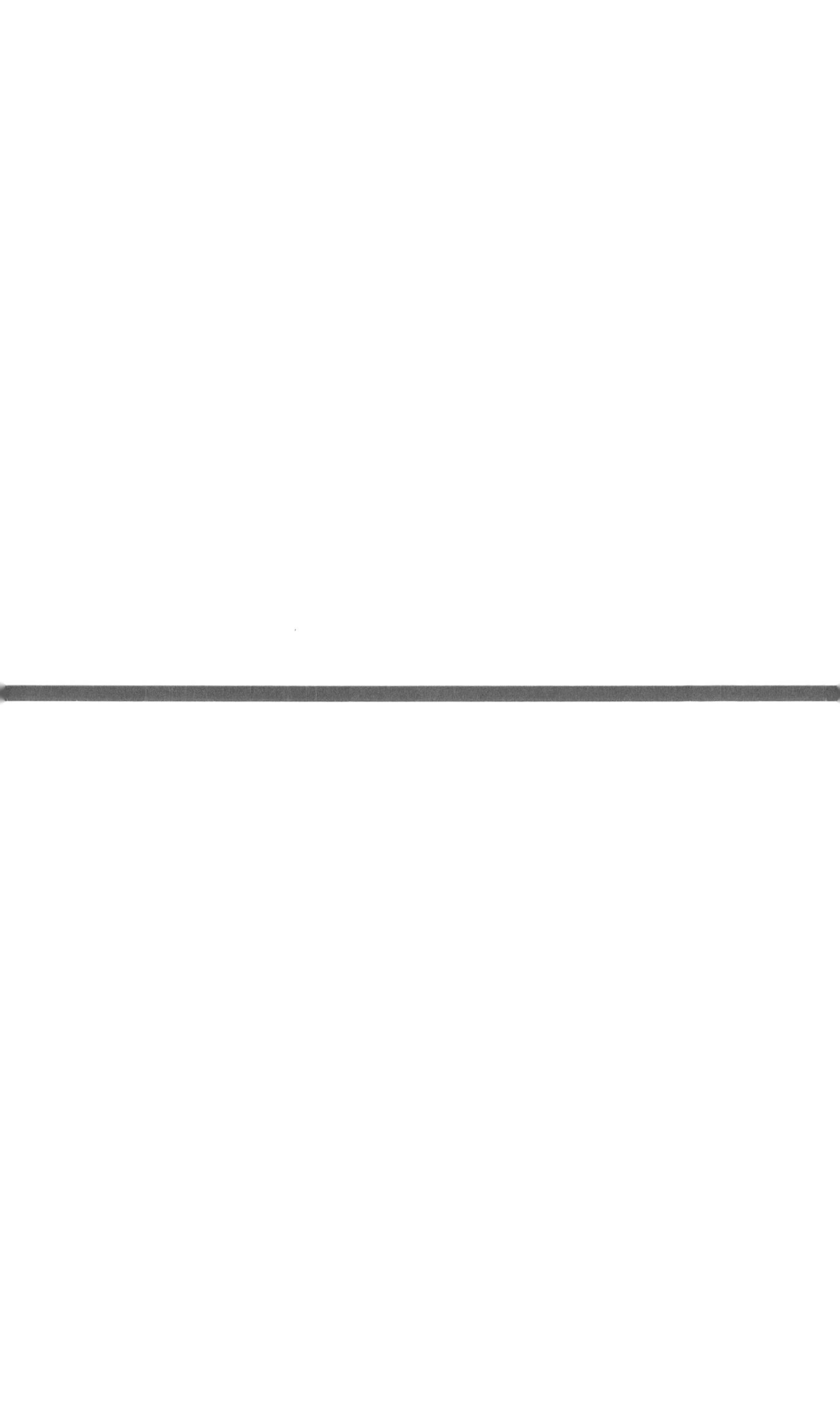

Contents

ONE - The Theologian as the Master Builder - 3

TWO - What is Psych Science? - 26

THREE - Areas and Subdisciplines of Psychological Science - 58

FOUR - Other Specialties - 119

Acknowledgements

This brief introduction of psychological science to theologians was written at the encouragement of Oliver Crisp in the context of our TheoPsych program, a John Templeton Foundation-funded effort to introduce theologians to the theories and findings of psychological science. Decisions about what to include here were importantly shaped by discussions with the many participants in that program to whom I am grateful. In addition to Oliver, I am also grateful to the entire TheoPsych team for their work on the program and their encouragement and input on this primer: Rebecca Dorsey (co-project leader), Kutter Callaway, Sarey Martin Concepción, Allison Wiltshire, and Holly Crain. I am thankful, too, that our TheoPsych scientific contributors have helped inform the kinds of topics and illustrations that I have used here. For their contributions to the TheoPsych program, I thank my colleagues Tyler Greenway, Mark McMinn, Sarah Schnitker, Erin Smith, and especially Mari Clements, Bob

Emmons, Pete Hill, Pam King, Lindsey Root Luna, Brad Strawn, and Bill Newsome.

Several psych scientists and theologians provided feedback on the first complete draft and offered numerous illustrations and citations for key psychological work and also theological projects that have productively drawn upon psychological science. I am grateful for the valuable advice of Michael Burdett, Laird Edman, Joanna Leidenhag, Erin Kidd, Mark McMinn, Sarah Lane Ritchie, Lindsey Root Luna, Jonathan Rutledge, Erin Smith, Chris Woznicki, and Simeon Zahl. Erin Smith's contributions were considerable throughout, but substantive enough in the sections on social psychology and sensitive periods in developmental psychology that they rise to the level of co-authorship of those sections (which I have footnoted at those points in the text).

This book was created under the editorial guidance of Blueprint 1543's director of communications Sarey Martin Concepción. In addition to this primer, Sarey has produced and assembled a wonderful range of resources for theologians to continue their education in psychological science. These resources are gathered into courses at TheoPsych Academy, available at theopsych.com:

theopsych.com

ONE
The Theologian as the Master Builder

Imagine being the chief builder of a large and lavish palace. The monarch commissioning the building demands the finest in form and function. The artistry must be unrivaled. To complete this extravagant project, you will need the contributions of many workers common for grand residences such as framers, masons, plumbers, electricians, finish carpenters, and painters. But because of the demand for unsurpassed beauty and utility, you may need to bring in specialists who hail from regions of the world that have cultivated relevant architectural engineering and arts to the highest degree. As an experienced builder, you know how to coordinate a team of craftspeople to complete a job with excellence, but the particular demands of this palace will force you to incorporate experts and their skills with which you have little or no experience. How will you find and vet these experts? When will their skills be needed in the building process? How can you effectively coordinate their work with that of the others, especially when yours will be an international, multicultural, and multilingual team?

In some ways, a theologian's task can be like this master builder's. Theologians, too, may find themselves needing to draw upon many tools of intellectual inquiry to construct a unified treatment of a theological question. Historical, linguistic, literary, and philosophical contributions commonly find a role in theology. But today more tools of inquiry are available to theologians, particularly the human and social sciences such as anthropology, archaeology, psychology, and sociology. Depending upon the particular area of theology, behavioral ecology, cosmology, neuroscience, and many other science specialties may have a contribution to make. How, then, do theologians know when to bring in contributions from a particular scientific domain and how do they do it well? Figuratively, where should they go to find the best artisans to help build the palace and how can theologians communicate with those specialists and facilitate them becoming part of the team of builders, unified under a common purpose?

The aim of this book is to help theologians understand enough about psychological science to know when it is that these scientists and their skills might make a helpful contribution to a theological project. Not every building project needs a marble-worker and not every theological project needs contributions from the psychological sciences, but likewise, as marble-work done well may add strength, beauty, and value to a home, psychological science has promise to enhance a theological project.

For builders to properly incorporate marble-work into a structure, it helps to know enough about the properties and limitations of marble. And before inviting a marble-working specialist onto a building site, it may be helpful for the master builder to know something about the work style and needs of a marble-worker. Similarly, this book is meant to introduce theologians to psychological science — what it is and some of its potential contributions to theology — and to the general character of psychological scientists — how they approach their work.

My intended audience is theologians who are already open to the possibility of psychological science helping them in their theological scholarship and application but who may want a little guidance initially. I wish to encourage them that they are on the right track but also make it easier to see when psychological science might be of greatest value. If I can also encourage theologians who are a bit more suspicious about bringing psychological science onto their building sites, to give psych science some fresh consideration, all the better.

I wonder if even theologians positively disposed toward psychological science as a craftsperson on their building site might underestimate this science's potential in bringing some new tools to theological problems. It would be easy to think that, for instance, because psych science is about humans, only practical theology or theological anthropology are likely to enjoy benefit from psych science perspectives. Or because the sciences help us better read "the book of nature" or understand "general revelation" that "the book of scripture" or "special revelation" must remain segregated from any psych science discoveries. In many specific cases this is likely true. Nonetheless, with some imagination and, perhaps some progress in the psychological sciences spurred on by theological questions, psych science can be useful to theologians working on a very broad range of topics.

Even if one's focus is on what can be extracted from special revelation, not general revelation, and the topic of interest isn't directly about human nature or human restoration, psych science may still have something to offer. Elsewhere I have argued that divine revelation — including special revelation — is a particularly apt place for psych science to contribute.[1] After all, at its core, divine revelation is God's *communication to* humans concerning who God is, what kind of relationship God wants with them, and how that relationship can be cultivated. Successful communication does something to change the thoughts and feelings in the minds of the audience. It follows that psychological science — science that concerns itself with thoughts, feelings, and behaviors — may have something useful to offer the study of revelation. Alister McGrath notes:

> Revelation may involve the interpretation of historical events, the hearing of the word of God, the reading of Scripture, experience of the presence of God, or reflection on the natural world . . . As John of Damascus stressed in the eighth century, revelation does not circumvent the natural, material world; the incarnation

1 Barrett, J. L. (2021). "Revelation and cognitive science: An invitation." In B. Mezei, F. Murphy, & K. Oakes (eds.), *Oxford Handbook of Divine Revelation*, pp. 518-536. Oxford University Press. For a theological account of divine accommodation that draws upon cognitive science concerning "embodied cognition," see Tanton (2021). Accommodating Embodied Thinkers. *Modern Theology*, 37, 316-335. doi: 10.1111/moth.12685.

> represents an extension and confirmation, not a contradiction, of earlier modes of revelation. Yet that process of interpretation and appropriation also includes human perception, which simply cannot be eliminated for the sake of theological convenience.[2]

Or as Tobias Tanton has argued:

> If the incarnation— the central act of God's revelation in Christian salvation history—can be understood in terms of accommodation, then it is only a small step further to think of accommodation as a category of theological epistemology. Accommodation thus becomes a condition for any and all theological knowledge: if humans are to hear and to understand God's revelation, it must be mediated in a way which is comprehensible to them.[3]

Psychological science, in the service of theological inquiry, can help shore up our understanding of the human side of divine revelation. And because divine revelation is the common source for theology, psych science has the potential to make contributions, even if modest ones, in many areas of theology.

Where I am Coming from

This primer concerns psychological science written by a psychological scientist. I am not a philosopher, historian, or sociologist of psychological science and the claims I make here are not meant to carry the authority of experts

2 McGrath, A. (2008). *The Open Secret: A New Secret for Natural Theology*. Blackwell. p. 108.

3 Tanton (2021), p. 318.

with those specializations. Rather, my aim is to serve as a native guide to my community, as I have experienced them. I draw upon my roughly 30 years being part of this group of scientists, but one who has done scholarship on the scientific study of religious thought and the implications of this scientific inquiry. Hence, I have also collegially interacted and sometimes collaborated with non-scientists. These interactions have helped me see my home discipline through others' eyes. Collaborating with philosophers, theologians, and religious studies scholars, and being part of an anthropology faculty and later on the faculty of a theological institution, has helped me recognize more clearly the peculiar features of psychological science, especially in contrast with the humanities. Teaching graduate students of psychology how to integrate their theology and lived faith with their work as emerging psychologists has also been helpful to me in identifying where the points of friction may be.

I offer this personal contextualization so that you, the reader, know where I am coming from and can adjust your expectations accordingly. But I also share these details because I am conscious of the fact that for nearly every general claim that I offer about how I have come to know psychological science, it would be possible to find exceptions or counter-points. The scientific study of human psychology is a dynamic, diverse, and global enterprise. My experience will not match everyone else's and my view of this area of scientific inquiry is from a particular perspective.

What is Psychological Science?

If psychological science were a geographical region, I would say something like, "Psychological Science is a border region of the nation-state known as Psychology. Though populated in part by immigrants from neighboring nations such as Neuroscience, Linguistics, Education, and Artificial Intelligence, those living in the region of Psychological Science primarily identify as Psychologists. This national identity is much more important professionally and personally than their regional identity as scientists. Conversely, this particular region in Psychology has had an over-sized influence on all of the nation of Psychology. Those studying psychology – even if they will never do any actual science themselves – are trained in the epistemology and methods of scientific inquiry. They are taught (sometimes unsuccessfully) to value scientific methods as the preeminent way to understand what is true within the domain of psychology." And yet, saying that "psychology is a science" is a bit like saying "ministry is theology"; it isn't completely untrue, but misses some important emphases in lived realities.

Psychological science is the scientific study of human thought and behavior. Fundamentally it is a mode of inquiry. Only secondarily (and transiently) is it a body of findings and theories. The facts of the matter, as in many areas of the sciences, are often contested and under constant revision, but typically in a cumulative and progressive sense. The findings of the past rarely are simply discarded but become part of the growing body of evidence for which new theories must account. Amidst the flux of ever-changing findings and theories, the unifying thread of psychological science is a focus on thought and behavior of humans and sometimes other animals (but usually to better illuminate our understanding of humans), and the use of scientific methods for engaging this study. Psychological scientists are constantly looking for the causes and consequences (psychological and otherwise) of human thought and behavior and use scientific methods as their primary mode. I will say more about what they mean by "scientific" below, but at its core, psychological scientists seek to make claims on the basis of behaviors that have been systematically observed in such a manner that another could, in principle, replicate these observations and arrive at similar conclusions about the facts of the matter. Inductive logic and mathematics (typically statistics) are valued tools. In a nutshell, that is psychological science.

Psychology, however, is a much broader category. Many people who identify as psychologists are not in the business of doing scientific inquiry but may be putting into practice the findings of psychological science to address some real-world problems; for instance, helping people navigate life's stressors, improve their decision-making, create more efficient organizations,[4] or teach children more effectively.[5] And some psychologists either tacitly or actively reject the alleged preeminence of psychological science. That is, they study human thought and behavior without using scientific methods, but instead use deductive methods to draw inferences from the writings of great thinkers, or they base their claims on their own personal observations and introspections that are not available to others

4 Psychological scientists study matters concerning organizational dynamics and effective leadership as well as what makes for strong work environments. Much of this practical science is part of the subfield known as industrial-organizational psychology. It is easy to suppose that insights from this subfield could be helpful for ministry organizations and even local churches.

5 Do our methods of catechism, youth services, etc. teach effectively, given what we know about human cognitive and motivational dynamics?

as data sources.[6] Some who identify as psychologists are not trying to make new discoveries or apply the findings of psychological science, but instead are "psychologists" by virtue of being mental health professionals. Not every physician is a medical scientist, not every farmer is a botanist, not every engineer is a physicist, not every minister is a theologian, and not every psychologist is a psychological scientist. Because of how broad and diverse the categories "psychology" and "psychologists" are, I will primarily use the terms *psychological science* and *psychological scientist* for greater precision, and *psych science* and *psych scientist* for greater economy.

Even the category *psychological science* is extremely broad. Wherever humans are and whatever they are doing, there is psychological science to be done because humans are constantly thinking and behaving. In the scientific study of human thought and behavior, "thought" is construed very broadly. It includes sensations, perceptions, feelings, intuitions, propositions, decisions, reflections, imaginings, inferences, categorizations, attributions, and many other mental activities. Likewise, "behavior" may include speech acts, eye-movements, sweating, breathing, pointing, walking, or even the firing of a single neuron. With enough creativity and measurement precision, observable behaviors can be used to make inferences about the enormous range of different mental processes. Making inferences to the quality and dynamics of some phenomenal states must be done with great care, but it can be and is done. If there

6 For instance, occasionally scholars will take for granted particular models of human minds developed by luminaries such as Sigmund Freud, Carl Jung, or Carl Rogers – even if elements of these models rest on shaky scientific foundations – and then deductively speculate about a Freudian, Jungian, Rogerian (etc.) perspective on this or that. This practice is not what I mean by *psychological science*.

is a domain of human experience that someone claims is "unmeasurable," a psych scientist might reply, "Not with that attitude!"[7]

> Though psychological science emphasizes minds (*psyches*) and, hence, individual thought and action, how individuals interact with each other and with broader cultural-level patterns would also be included under the umbrella term *psychological science*. For this reason, the psych science(s) that I wish to capture may also be performed by non-psychologists. Any scholar who uses scientific methods to investigate the mental states and behaviors of individual humans could contribute to psych science, including anthropologists, archaeologists, behavioral scientists, cognitive scientists, linguists, neuroscientists, sociologists, and even experimental philosophers.

7 I don't mean to say anything is measurable. Of course not. Sometimes measurement only partially or indirectly indexes some phenomenon of interest to a theologian. Nonetheless, psych science is old enough now to tell us that a little optimism and creativity can payoff. Even if a phenomenon of theological concern does not, ultimately, have measurable features, the exercise of trying to discover just what can and cannot be measured may be fruitful in better understanding the problem space.

Discerning When a Theologian may Benefit from Some Psych Science[8]

Because of its broad focus on human thought and behavior, psychological science can and does reach into many areas that also concern theologians. What is the nature of humans? How can sinful inclinations be inherited? What are the consequences on congregants of participating in Holy Communion one way rather than another? What are effective ways to teach children about the Gospel? Why does it often seem so hard for people to grasp and hold onto the idea of Grace?[9] What is the place of work and rest in a flourishing life? What are practical techniques for cultivating gratitude or humility? How does one forgive someone who has committed a horrible wrong? What does it look like to be "transformed by the renewing of your mind" (Rom. 12:2)? Answers to all of these questions, and many more like them, may, in principle, be informed by psychological science.

Theological questions commonly concern humanity's relationship to God, what it means to flourish and live the sort of lives God intends for us, and how the Church should go about advancing the Kingdom of God. Consequently, theological inquiry may advance more rapidly with an infusion of insights from the human sciences—perhaps *especially* the psychological sciences. But not *all* theological questions would benefit from an infusion of psych science. So when is it most likely that psych science could be

---

8 Much of the following section was first developed as a presentation for the TheoPsych seminar program hosted by Fuller Theological Seminary, and later was presented as a blog on the Logos Institute website of St Andrews University's School of Divinity (November 2019). https://blogos.wp.st-andrews.ac.uk

9 Emmons, R. A., Hill, P. C., Barrett, J. L., & Kapic, K. M. (2017). Psychological and theological reflections on grace and its relevance for science and practice. *Psychology of Religion and Spirituality*, 9(3), 276-284. http://doi.org/10.1037/rel0000136

helpful to theological inquiry? Four questions will aid this discernment process:

1. Are you (the theologian) making descriptive psychological claims?[10]
2. Are you making normative claims supported by descriptive psychological claims?
3. Are you making claims about what effects texts, rituals, and practices have on people?
4. Are you constructing an argument that uses intuitions as premises?

These four questions help to pick out different ways in which input from psych science – its findings and theories – may prove helpful for doing theology. These questions are not meant to be exhaustive or exclusive of each other. That is, it may be that even if the answer is "no" to all four of these questions that, with some creativity, psych science may still prove useful. And of course, a particular theological project may generate affirmative responses to more than one of these questions.

Are You Making Descriptive Psychological Claims?

Though much of theology is prescriptive or normative, in the course of doing theology, it is not uncommon to make descriptive psychological claims. These claims might concern mental states or how psychological processes work. Similarly, theologians sometimes describe psychological features of human nature. For instance, when Pope John

---

10 Here "psychological claims" are claims about mental states and behaviors that, in principle, could be examined through empirical, scientific methods. Mental states include thoughts, feelings, attitudes, beliefs, percepts, and sensations. And whereas it may be argued that even mundane descriptive claims contain some tacit normative content, it is not helpful to pretend that these largely descriptive claims from psych science are equivalent to the explicitly normative claims common in theology.

Paul II wrote in his 1998 encyclical letter *Fides et Ratio,* "In the far reaches of the human heart there is a seed of desire and nostalgia for God" (p. 15), he was making an empirically tractable, descriptive claim about human psychology. In principle, psych science could seek evidence for this alleged desire and nostalgia.[11]

Similarly, it is not uncommon for theologians to ask and attempt to answer questions that concern topics in psych science. For instance, in his book *Theology: The Basics*, Alister McGrath structures his presentation around the Apostle's Creed. Hence, he begins with the questions, "What does it mean to talk about 'believing in God'? What are we to understand by words such as 'belief' and 'faith'?"[12] These two questions are decidedly theological but simultaneously psychological. Psych scientists – along with other cognitive scientists – study what beliefs are, how they are formed, how they function, and how they change. Though "faith" is rarely used as a concept in psych science, it concerns several domains of psychological research because it has mental, motivational, and relational dimensions. Put another way, a theological treatment of "faith" could be informed and enriched by insights from psychological science (and vice versa).

---

11 Research in the cognitive science of religion may be moving close to such an exploration (see, for instance, Clark & Barrett (2010) concerning the *sensus divinitatis*. Clark, K. J., & Barrett, J. L. (2010). Reformed epistemology and the cognitive science of religion. *Faith & Philosophy*, 27(2), 174-189.
Furthermore, the psych science of human mental and emotional states may provide resources for thinking about how to characterize (or not) God's mental and emotional states, especially God the Son as Jesus of Nazareth. For instance, to what degree are such attributions to God problematically anthropomorphic instead of serving as helpful analogies? Gregory Peterson suggests such applications in his *Minding God: Theology and the Cognitive Sciences* (2002, Fortress Press).

12 McGrath, A. (2018). *Christian Theology: An Introduction*, Sixth Edition. Wiley Blackwell. p. 1.

When theologians do wish to make descriptive claims that have psychological content or dimensions, psychological science could be useful in reframing, supporting, nuancing, or challenging these claims.

Are You Making Normative Claims Supported by Psychological Claims?

Much of theology extends beyond discussions of what *is* the case to what *should be* the case. Typically, it would be folly to simply import the descriptive claims from psychological science into theology as normative claims. Just because people tend to think in a certain way does not mean they *should* think in such a way. Nevertheless, the descriptive claims of the sciences can play a role in theologically normative claims as premises in more complex arguments. For instance, the idea that most humans have no volitional control over the content of their dreams may reasonably bear upon whether one judges that people are morally culpable for their dream content. Likewise, as the consequences of thought or action may bear upon the value of that way of thought or action, understanding the likely consequences of the thought or action may matter to normative claims. If psychological science can demonstrate that feeling compassion toward an individual makes one more likely to treat that person kindly, and treating others kindly is to be commended, then learning to feel compassion toward others may also be commended. Likewise, if a particular virtue or attitude is commended on theological grounds, psych science could help reverse-engineer the means by which such goods could be cultivated in individuals. When making normative claims, there may be ways in which descriptive psychological claims could support, challenge, or nuance those normative claims.

In his book *Was Jesus God?* Richard Swinburne includes a section entitled "Christian Moral Teaching." In this section, as part of a discussion of why certain "supererogatory" behaviors (or behaviors that go beyond an expected "call of duty") seem to become "obligatory," we find the following text:

> Someone who has saved the satisfaction of sexual desire for a spouse will be able to regard and be regarded by that spouse as uniquely their own. And it is plausible to suppose that, if people get used to having casual sex before marriage, it becomes more natural to commit adultery when the marriage becomes difficult or boring; and it is also highly plausible to suppose that the example of many people abstaining from sexual intercourse before marriage will influence others to take their marriages more seriously.[13]

Notice that Swinburne makes several empirical suggestions about human thought and behavior. Is there a link between pre-marital chastity and attitudes toward a spouse being regarded as "uniquely their own"? Do people who have more frequent casual sex before marriage also find it more "natural to commit adultery when the marriage becomes difficult"? Does a culture of abstinence influence others to "take their marriages more seriously"? With a

---

13 Swinburne, R. (2008). *Was Jesus God?* Oxford University Press, p. 71.

little bit of effort, each of these claims could be translated into testable psych science research questions for which evidence may already be available. This evidence might strengthen, weaken, or otherwise qualify what Swinburne finds plausible.

Are You Making Claims About What Effects Texts, Rituals, and Practices Have on People?

It can be powerful and efficient rhetoric to talk about what worship does to worshippers, what a wedding does to those joined, or what prayers of thanksgiving do to those praying. Note, however, that this kind of language is often shorthand for a psychological claim. Take these examples from J. I. Packer's discussion of images of God in his book *Knowing God*:

> In a similar way the pathos of the crucifix obscures the glory of Christ, for it hides the fact of His deity, His victory on the cross, and His present kingdom. It displays His human weakness, but it conceals His divine strength; it depicts the reality of His pain, but keeps out of our sight the reality of His joy and His power.[14]
>
> Images *mislead men*. They convey false ideas about God. The very inadequacy with which they represent Him perverts our thoughts of Him, and plants in our minds errors of all sorts about His character and will.[15]

14 Packer, J. I. (1973). *Knowing God*. InterVarsity Press, p. 40-41.

15 Packer, 1973, p. 41

Packer speaks as if the crucifix or images of God *do* things to people: they obscure, display, conceal, mislead, and convey. These verbs all suggest that images have some sort of agency, which is useful but imprecise. In fact, it is humans who respond to images in particular ways. Humans perceive in images this or that. At best, images are stimuli for humans to think or respond in certain ways. Perhaps the artist or sculpture intends to communicate particular ideas and feelings through the image. In any case, human interactions with a crucifix or other image of the divine are psychological processes subject to potential psychological investigation. That is, psychological science could demonstrate (or falsify) that people who spend time gazing upon crucifixes are inclined to "forget" Jesus' deity, perhaps more readily associating him with human weakness and suffering rather than power and dominion. Perhaps some (but not all) images communicate God's transcendent properties *more* effectively than words. Packer has made numerous assertions that may be testable through psychological science.[16]

When discussing religious practices, rituals, disciplines, images, and so forth theologians may want to consider whether they are importing assumptions about psychological dynamics that may be adjusted and honed through engagement with psychological science.

16 Indeed, one of my first scholarly, psychological publications was inspired by just these claims of Packer. And so, sometimes theological treatments can encourage psych science, too. This study suffered from a very small sample size and so I regard its findings as very tentative and in need of more rigorous replication. Barrett, J. L. & VanOrman, B. (1996). The effects of image use in worship on God concepts. *Journal of Psychology and Christianity*, 15(1), 38-45.

Arguments about Affective Salience by Simeon Zahl

Simeon Zahl argues that the history of theology features many arguments that feature psychological claims, particularly the emotional and experiential consequences of doctrines. He writes:

What I mean by arguments about "affective salience" are theological arguments that focus on the practical emotional valence and the anticipated experiential impact of doctrines. A typical example of this phenomenon can be found in the disagreement between John Calvin and the authors of the Decree on Justification at the Council of Trent on the issue of election and assurance. In his argument in favor of predestination in the Institutes, Calvin asserts from the start that the value of the doctrine is not least that through it we come to "sincerely feel how much we are obliged to God." He argues that the doctrine should bestow upon those who understand and believe it "firmness and confidence" and "free[dom] from all fear." (Zahl, 37-38).

Calvin is making descriptive psychological claims in defense of a normative claim (i.e., that we should adopt predestination), and also making claims about the psychological consequences of believing such a doctrine. Calvin is not alone. Concerning John Wesley Zahl observes:

> *In a similar vein, John Wesley devotes half of his influential refutation of the doctrine of predestination (the sermon "Free Grace") to arguments about affective salience. According to Wesley, belief in the doctrine of predestination "has a manifest tendency to destroy holiness . . .for it wholly takes away those first motives to follow after it, [namely] the hope of future reward and fear of punishment"; it "naturally tends to inspire or increase a sharpness or eagerness of temper which is quite contrary to the meekness of Christ"; it "destroy[s] the comfort of religion, the happiness of Christianity"; and finally those who "hold this doctrine" often experience "a return of doubt and fears concerning [their] election and perseverance." (Zahl, p. 38, footnote 88).*
>
> In principle, empirical evidence could be marshalled that bears upon Calvin's and Wesley's claims concerning the emotional and experiential impact of these doctrinal positions.
>
> Zahl, S. (2020). *The Holy Spirit and Christian Experience.* Oxford University Press.

Are You Constructing an Argument that Uses Intuitions as Premises?

A fourth occasion in which psychological science could be useful to theologians is when an argument is strengthened by premises that are rooted in a theologian's own intuitions that they assume to be shared with their audiences. In this case, it is the theologian's intuitions themselves—*whether or not* these intuitions are *about* psychological states or dynamics—that could benefit from some scientific scrutiny. Intuitions are, after all, psychological states that relevant psychological science could investigate. Sometimes, this investigation could bear on the strength of these intuitions as premises in a theological argument.

The philosophical study of ethics has undergone a minor revolution in recent decades by the discovery that certain intuitions that philosophers had taken for granted in their arguments were irregularly shared by the general population, or even varied considerably across cultures. In some cases, the framing of thought experiments has been shown to shape key intuitions in ways that the strict logic of the thought problem was supposed to prevent. Perhaps most famous in this regard is the *Knobe Effect*. Joshua Knobe found that when an actor in an ethical thought problem brings about an unintended negative consequence through his or her actions, readers are very likely to judge the actor as morally blameworthy. Hence, a businessperson who tries to maximize profits but makes a particular decision that, as a byproduct, harms the environment, he or she is still judged as blameworthy for the action. Intuitions of relatively educated Americans seem fairly uniform in this regard. Nevertheless, when the actor performed the same action, driven by the same profit motives, and a *positive* byproduct was the unintended consequence (e.g., improving the environment), the action was not then judged to be praiseworthy, even though the relationship between the actor's intentions and the actor's desired outcomes was identical to the negative case. The Knobe Effect is the name of this asymmetry, and it was discovered by use of psych science methods.[17] It shows that the framing of a thought-problem can change normative intuitions. Thus, in many cases, the intuitions that philosophers have taken to be secure premises in their arguments may be fundamentally conditioned by their context, culture, or individual psychology. The area of "experimental philosophy" has developed to investigate these matters.[18]

The extension to theological ethics is straightforward. Insofar as theologians working on various projects develop arguments that rely upon what seems to be the case in particular situations, these "seemings" are potentially investigable using psychological science, as I described in relation to Swinburne's argument above.

To further illustrate, McGrath presents three different models for thinking about God as creator and briefly evaluates their relative strengths and weaknesses. In discussing the "artistic expression" model, part of the proposed strength of such a model includes the claim that, "There is also a natural link between the concept of creation as 'artistic expression' and the highly significant concept of 'beauty'".[19] It may seem fair enough that, indeed, a "natural link" exists between these two concepts, but is that intuition

---

17 Note, however, that this effect may be related to how irregular considerations of intentions are in judging the praise- and blameworthiness of actions across cultures and situations. For instance, Joseph Henrich suggests that elevated attention to intuitions is a consequence of peculiar cultural conditions, those in which most Western scholars live and work. Henrich, J. (2019). *The Weirdest People on Earth: How the West Became Psychologically Peculiar and Particularly Prosperous*. Farrar, Straus and Giroux.

18 For a review of the Knobe Effect and experimental philosophy as applied to morality, see https://plato.stanford.edu/entries/experimental-moral/. For an introduction to experimental philosophy by field leaders Joshua Knobe and Shaun Nichols, see https://plato.stanford.edu/archives/win2017/entries/experimental-philosophy/

19 McGrath, 2018, p. 48.

accurate and stable? I may be inclined to believe it, but is that because I have been culturally conditioned to link artistic expression with beauty instead of, say, awe, fear, or sublimity? A psychological investigation of these intuitions may reveal that arguments in favor of the "artistic expression" model over, the "emanation",[20] or "construction"[21] models are stronger in some populations as opposed to others. Perhaps, too, scientific consideration of intuitions concerning artistic expression and beauty would reveal additional reasons for favoring the artistic expression model. Perhaps we do readily connect beauty to the goodness of its creator, and as a result we may think of God's creative act as artistic expression which not only casts focus on beauty, it thereby helps us to consider God's goodness. It's possible, too, that attending to natural beauty also prompts a deeper appreciation of God's awesome power and untamed agency. Psychological science could help theologians develop or problematize such arguments. It may be that the time is right for developing an *experimental theology* that parallels experimental philosophy.[22]

The point is not that intuitions are not legitimate evidence in theological (or philosophical) arguments. Using intuitions is indispensable. How could we even marshal an argument without the intuition that our reasoning regarding

20 McGrath, 2018, p. 46.

21 McGrath, 2018, p. 47.

22 Philosopher Ian Church is leading a major John Templeton Foundation-funded initiative that seeks to begin such a development via experimental philosophy of religion. For instance, the problem of evil — whether an all-powerful, all-knowing, perfectly good God is consistent with the degree of evil in the world — may be an interesting illustrative case for bringing psych science methods to philosophy of religion problems (e.g. Church, I. M., Carlson, R., and Barrett, J. L. (2020). Evil Intuitions? The Problem of Evil, Experimental Philosophy, and the Need for Psychological Research. *Journal of Psychology and Theology*). For more about this new initiative, here is an interview with Ian Church: https://soundcloud.com/radiofreehillsdale/ian-church-launching-experimental-philosophy-of-religion

the argument is on the right track?[23] The point is that sometimes our intuitions – even carefully inspected ones – can be less stable than we imagine or can even mislead us.

To reiterate, four questions may be helpful to theologians in discerning whether some psychological science will enhance the palace they are building. Are you (1) making descriptive psychological claims; (2) making normative claims supported by psychological claims; (3) making claims about what effects texts, rituals, and practices have on people; and/or (4) constructing an argument that uses intuitions as premises? Of course, it will be much easier for theologians to confidently and accurately answer these questions—especially the first two—if they have a stronger sense for the range of "psychological claims." In the following chapters I provide a whirlwind tour of psych science.

23 I thank Jonathan Rutledge for observing that any intellectual inquiry begins with at least a tacit assumption or intuition of self-trust.

TWO
What is Psych Science?[24]

A Very Brief History
A Young Science

Psychological science is about the same age as the automobile and the telephone, just a little younger than Canada and a bit older than Australia. Or, to put it on a theological timeline, psych science was "born" only seven years before Karl Barth and Paul Tillich. It is common to mark the start of psychological science with the establishment of Wilhelm Wundt's laboratory in Germany in 1879. Wundt used systematic measurements of people's self-reported mental states to attempt to understand the dynamics of thought processes. Though the reliance on self-reported states and introspection fell out of favor in subsequent decades, due

24 See Myers & DeWall (2018), inside front and back covers for "The Story of Psychology: A Timeline" by C. L. Brewer, and also the Prologue for more historical details and a general overview. Myers, D. G. & DeWall, C. N. (2018). *Psychology, 12th edition*. Worth Publishers.

to their lack of reliability, Wundt's work indicated a shift to more systematic, observational methods for studying human mental processes than the largely analytic or anecdote-driven studies that characterized most previous studies of the mind. With infusions of methods and insights from physiology and behavioral sciences, psychological science began to become distinguished from its primary parent discipline, philosophy, in the decades before and after the start of the twentieth century.[25]

The youthfulness of psychological science shows in how many findings and theories are contested and, as a result, how dynamic it is. Physics, chemistry, and biology have had much more time to amass larger bodies of well-established findings that the preponderance of scientists would agree are basically settled knowledge. In psych science, even many of the findings that the field holds with great confidence may be the subject of further scrutiny and extension, especially into new populations. After all, unlike the properties of the oxygen atom, we cannot simply take for granted that the properties of, say, concept formation are essentially the same in Switzerland, Sri Lanka, and Swaziland.

A Development of Subject Matter

Psych Science's brief history has seen considerable disagreement over what its subject matter is, beginning with mental states and behaviors, narrowing to only behaviors,

25 Both psychology and philosophy claim William James as one of their own. James is commonly known as the father of American psychology. Probably James' most discussed work in contemporary psychology remains his *The Varieties of Religious Experience* (1902, Longmans, Green & Co.), which was adapted from his Gifford Lectures in natural theology.

and then broadening again. Wundt's work was quickly followed by Ivan Pavlov's landmark studies of how dogs come to associate sounds or touches with the arrival of food and, so, can learn to salivate at the sound of a bell or buzzer. This work was elaborated by John Watson and Rosalie Rayner into what is known as Pavlovian or classical conditioning.[26] Classical conditioning is the process by which organisms learn to react to a new (conditioned) stimulus similar to a previous (unconditioned) stimulus. The success of this research program to generate measurable, replicable findings in contrast with the more speculative and evasive claims of Sigmund Freud and others concerning conscious and unconscious mental states, encouraged psych science to focus on behaviors instead of mental states and processes. The resulting *behaviorism* was the dominant perspective in psych science up until the 1960s. B.F. Skinner was the twentieth century's champion of behaviorism. His studies of operant conditioning, how human and animal behavior could be modified through systems of rewards and punishments, led to some heady conclusions that *all* of human behavior could be understood as the product of various basic learning mechanisms that humans share with other animals. For much of the twentieth century psych science was primarily the study of behavior, not thought.

But behaviorisms preeminence began to visibly fracture in the 1950s and 60s with a number of new findings that undercut the model of human minds as simple learning machines. For instance, in the 1960s, John Garcia

26 For a fun overview of behaviorism, see *The Crash Course: Psychology, episode 11*: https://www.youtube.com/watch?v=qG2SwE_6uVM. See also Myers & DeWall (2018), Chapter 7.

demonstrated that some associations between a new stimulus and a behavioral response could be formed after a single exposure to the new stimulus, even if the aversive response (such as nausea) arises hours after the stimulus.[27] Formally known as the *Garcia Effect*, I like to call this the "cheeseburger effect" because once, after getting carsick on a road trip after having eaten a cheeseburger, I felt slightly nauseated even thinking about a cheeseburger for about a decade thereafter. Garcia's line of research demonstrated that animals—including human animals—show *preparedness* toward some learning over others. Similarly, humans and other primates have been shown to easily and rapidly form a fear of snakes.[28] It was beginning to look as though simple learning mechanisms were insufficient to predict human behavior. Some built-in predilections to learn or think certain things instead of others better accounted for the evidence, opening the door to reconsider the place of mental representations, perception, and thought processes in psych science.

It isn't that the study of mental processes wasn't part of psych science at all until the mid-twentieth century. One can find important studies of cognitive development (e.g., Jean Piaget) and memory (e.g., F. C. Bartlett) dating to the 1920s and 30s. But it took failures in the behaviorist paradigm, the growth of more systematic, quantitative, and (thus) "scientific" studies of mental states and processes, and new metaphors from artificial computing machines to

---

27 Garcia, J. & Koelling, R. A. (1966). Relation of cue to consequence in avoidance learning. *Psychonomic Science*, 4, 123-124.

28 Öhman, A., & Mineka, S. (2001). Fears, phobias, and preparedness: Toward an evolved module of fear and fear learning. *Psychological Review*, 108(3), 483-522. https://doi.org/10.1037/0033-295X.108.3.483

create space for a psych science that unflinchingly included the study of thought (perception, attitudes, decision-making, etc.) as part of its mainstream. The interdisciplinary space called *cognitive science* draws upon the cognitive wing of psychological science as well as artificial intelligence, cognitive anthropology, linguistics, neuroscience, and philosophy (of mind, primarily).[29]

The 1950s and 60s, then, ushered in a "cognitive revolution" in psych science, which included Noam Chomsky's revolutionary studies concerning universal features of human language. Arguably this cognitive shift was encouraged by efforts to develop artificial intelligence in machines. How much could we learn about human thought and behavior if we re-conceptualized humans as complex biological machines that perform computations? Perhaps efforts to engineer artificial computers could inspire new insights concerning human computers.[30] Since the 1960s, then, psych science has generally accepted human behaviors and mental states and their operations as legitimate targets of inquiry.

---

29 It can be functionally difficult to distinguish between cognitive psychology and cognitive science much of the time as cognitive psychology is the largest contributor to this interdisciplinary space, The journal *Cognition* is a lead journal in both cognitive science and cognitive psychology.

30 Many scholars flinch at the idea of calling human minds computers and dismiss this talk as, at best, a metaphor. Strictly speaking, however, humans and other biological systems do computation and, hence, are literally computers on top of everything else they are. Those psych scientists who persist in using the language of computation are rarely naïve about the fact that how humans do computation is importantly different than how silicon-based microcomputers do computation. Exactly how they differ and how they are similar continues to generate new studies and insights.

A Refinement of Methods[31]

Not only is psych science's brief history characterized by a struggle over just what counts as its subject matter, but can also be seen as a development of research methods appropriate to that study. Sitting uneasily between the natural sciences and the social sciences, psych science has had to struggle with what counts as scientifically "legitimate" ways to study human thought and behavior. Introspection, unstructured observation and interviews, and case-studies relinquished much (but not all) ground to much more structured and controlled research methods, most notably, experimental methods. In recent years, experimental methods are starting to surrender some place of privilege to studies that use complex statistical methods for discerning patterns in human thought and behavior via large data sets such as those available through social media platforms. Psych scientists are constantly inventing research methods for investigating human thought and behavior.

At risk of oversimplifying, what holds these diverse methods together is a drive to maximize the reliability and validity of the measures used in a research protocol that is replicable by other research teams. Reliability, here, is the degree to which a measure will yield similar results when used repeatedly. For instance, a measure of a personality trait such as extraversion would have good reliability if the same person scores similarly at various points in the day, on various days of the week, and at different times of the year.

Validity concerns the extent to which a measure plausibly indexes the phenomenon it purports to measure. If

31 See also Myers & DeWall (2018), Preface and Chapter 1.

an "analytic intelligence test," for instance, does as good a job picking out professional logicians as it does Star Wars fans (with no particular logical acumen), then its validity is suspect. Validity is a multidimensional concept and, depending upon the type of measure being developed or used, it may be scrutinized in terms of internal and external validity, construct validity, face validity, ecological validity, and others.[32] Differences in the prioritization of various types of validity can dramatically shape research. However, the main point is that psych scientists are constantly wrestling over whether the measures and procedures that they use have appropriate rigor, that they will yield results in which we can have confidence. And sometimes that wrestling pits reliability and validity against each other. What looks like a "bad" measure to an outsider may actually be a strong and useful balancing of these various considerations.

Importantly, psych science values research that generates findings that other research teams could, at least in principle, replicate. Characteristics of the researcher — his or her historical and cultural situation or intellectual assumptions — should not be determining factors in the result of their study's findings. Psych science itself has compiled abundant evidence that humans are rather unreliable when it comes to accurately detecting patterns, protecting themselves from reasoning errors and faulty judgments, and neutralizing their own biases. It is for these reasons that psych scientists work so hard at scrutinizing and refining their research methods, and being very explicit about their measures, protocols, and analysis methods. Good practice

32 For a discussion of many dimensions of validity see: https://www.simplypsychology.org/validity.html

dictates that others should be able to re-run (or replicate) the study and get similar results. Indeed, psych scientists are commonly required by journals or professional associations to make their data available to other research teams for re-analysis as well.[33]

It is for these reasons that quantitative methods have become so important in psych science. A careful observer of human nature may accurately connect some causes and effects concerning human thought and action, but "folk wisdom" is also full of erroneous or under-supported conclusions. As Thomas Gilovich playfully summarizes, in his book *How We Know What Isn't So*, humans often "see" patterns where there aren't any.[34] Some of these are relatively benign such as finding backmasking in records or thinking full moons cause expectant mothers to go into labor. Others are more serious such as the *false consensus effect*, thinking that our own beliefs, values, and preferences are more widely shared than they are. Why does this happen? In part

---

33 Some readers may be familiar with the so-called "replication crisis" that has hit psychological and medical sciences in recent years. In brief, the challenge is that some prominent findings have failed to replicate upon re-examination. Partly this is a dynamic of continually trying to stretch our knowledge into new areas and characterizes many sciences to some degree. But it appears that in social psychology and some areas of medical science, the number of studies failing to replicate is disturbingly high. Should we regard this "crisis" as evidence that the methodological safeguards valued in these sciences are not working? I read this just the opposite way. Psych science continues to self-scrutinize to improve its methods and purge itself of suspect findings so that they don't continue to be propagated based upon faulty evidence. For instance, it is becoming increasingly common to "preregister" studies in advance of conducting them so that researchers can't simply fish through a dataset to make discoveries — a practice which increases the risk of spurious findings. It is important, too, to note that some "failures" to replicate are not failures at all, but highlight that some results are dependent upon specific conditions or population. Furthermore, not all areas of psych science have difficulty replicating findings. For more on this topic, see https://nobaproject.com/modules/the-replication-crisis-in-psychology.

34 A fun treatment of many of these reasoning biases and heuristics is social psychologist Thomas Gilovich's *How We Know What Isn't So* (1990). Many of these same psychological dynamics have been revisited by popular author Malcom Gladwell in *Blink: The Power of Thinking without Thinking* (2007, Back Bay Books).

because we are bad a keeping track of background probabilities and base rates (because to do so requires attending to non-events), calculating probabilities, and seeking out data-points that disconfirm our assumptions. For instance, how would we know whether full moons impact the rates of babies being born or crime rates? We can't just rely on the birth or crime notices during the full moon, but must attend to all crime or babies born during all moon phases. That isn't easy, and so we are inclined to rely on our impressions concerning how two variables (e.g., full moon and babies born) correspond. Likewise, how do we know whether BMW drivers really are the worst? We are inclined to notice every time we see a BMW driver misbehave but are far less likely to notice when they don't, or to attend to less distinctive models of cars' driving habits. Doing so is cognitively costly (and time consuming) and so we don't generally take the needed care to generate good evidence for establishing such patterns. Sometimes our native frequency tabulators get it right,[35] but not all the time. The scientific and quantitative methods of psych science drive researchers to reduce these reasoning errors.

Characterizing Psychological Scientists

Common Intellectual Dispositions

Psych science is a guild that is noteworthy for two common intellectual dispositions: curiosity and a somewhat suspicious, critical stance toward claims. Like many scholars, psychological scientists wonder why this or that is the case,

35 The BMW thing may have a basis in reality, even if this study is a bit, ahem, over-interpreted: https://jalopnik.com/science-confirms-that-bmw-and-prius-drivers-are-the-wor-1120783177

what causes people to behave this way or that, or what the consequences might be of a given feeling or attitude. They wonder whether apparent correlations between events are causally connected and, if so, how. In these ways psychological scientists are like many other scholars and especially other scientists. Scientists of many sorts are concerned with generating causal explanations for observable phenomena. As *psychological* scientists, however, this group of scientists often find their curiosity piqued by observing human behaviors, news headlines, conventional wisdom, adages, and aphorisms. And so, a study could be inspired by a saying such as "birds of a feather flock together." Studies could also be inspired by an experience or intuition. For instance, Yale cognitive and developmental psychologist Frank Keil once shared that a study he conducted was inspired by a power-outage that left his neighborhood without access to the Internet and the impression that everyone was getting dumber as a consequence. The resulting studies showed that people overestimate how much they know (and so feel smarter) when they have recently conducted a successful online search for information.[36] The experience of feeling "dumber" as the result of not having access to the Internet spawned a study of false intellectual confidence when one has access to the Internet.

Psychological scientists are a curious people concerning what others consider mundane. For the ordinary person the question, "Why do I think there is a coffee mug in my hand?," is absurd when one is holding a coffee mug.

---

36 Fisher, M., Goddu, M.K., & Keil, F.C. (2015). Searching for explanations: How the Internet inflates estimates of internal knowledge. *Journal of Experimental Psychology. General*. 144: 674-87. PMID 25822461 DOI: 10.1037/xge0000070

"Because there is a coffee mug in your hand," is a satisfactory answer. Not so for a typical psychological scientist. Just because something is the case is not an explanation for why it is that someone *thinks* it is the case. The psychological scientist may still wonder how it is that the sensory information concerning the coffee mug is processed to form a representation that is consciously accessible as a thought about a factual state of affairs. Under what conditions might such a belief about the coffee mug not arise? What role does one's personal past or developmental history play in populating a person's mind with representations that might be triggered by the visual and tactile information of holding a coffee mug? Psychological scientists are curious about the details of how people think and how thoughts might (or might not) generate behaviors and vice versa, even in domains that seem "obvious" or trivial.

This curiosity — even in the seemingly mundane features of human experience — is piqued in part because of a second intellectual disposition, a sort of skeptical realism. Generally, psychological scientists, like most natural scientists, are committed to the existence of a knowable real world that includes human beings. But perhaps especially because they study human thought, they are suspicious of claims concerning human thought and behavior that aren't backed up by sufficient observable evidence gathered in a way that minimizes or accounts for idiosyncratic perspectives, biases, and assumptions. Psychological science itself has demonstrated repeatedly that individual humans are subject to misperceiving, misremembering, misunderstanding, and mis-reasoning so often as to cast doubt on many claims made only on the basis of personal experience, introspection, anecdote, or the testimony of others, including the testimony of experts.[37] And so, just because something is conventional wisdom or the consensus of experts, or even plain to one's senses, this[38] does not mean that that thing can be accepted without further scrutiny. Even commonplace observations, then, can be prompts for more research; the obvious is the beginning of inquiry and not the end.

Because human thought is often untrustworthy as a sure guide to truth, psychological scientists constantly demand replicable evidence: evidence gathered in such a way that someone else could replicate the study and obtain similar results. For this reason, psychological scientists often have chilly relationships with scholars in neighboring guilds who are not as self-suspicious. A strong ethnography, generated by a social anthropologist could be a wellspring of new hypotheses for a psychological scientist but rarely would be taken to settle a question about how and why a particular people think and act as they do. Similarly, a careful historical analysis purporting to explain how the ideas of a particular leader influenced subsequent behaviors in others would probably be taken as merely suggestive unless it explicitly drew upon psychological science research to fortify the analysis.

Early in its history, psychological science relied on

---

37 Psychologist Erin Smith cleverly applies these observations to attitudes Christians may hold toward the sciences. Smith, E. I. (2020). The role of psychology in advancing dialogue between science and Christianity. *Perspectives on Science and Christian Faith*, 72(4), 204-221.

38 I thank Erin Smith for this example that many will remember due to the social media turbulence it created: https://www.wired.com/2015/02/science-one-agrees-color-dress/.

introspection, case studies, anecdotes, and thoughtful analyses as means to answer almost all questions that might qualify as "psychological." But these techniques are insufficiently able to address all questions in the purview of psych science. Thus, with a wider variety of rigorous scientific and quantitative approaches, modern psych science has a wider array to methods that can be better matched to specific questions. Psychological science of today looks very different than it did 100 years ago. Current practices of psychological science have been honed over time to reduce measurement errors and hasty interpretations and generalizations, even if they can never be entirely eliminated.[39] A strong emphasis on quantification and the use of statistics help guard against these errors.

The suspicious nature of psychological scientists is not just a caution to theologians wishing to engage this tribe but a potential resource as well. A theologian who makes a claim about human nature — particularly one that concerns how humans are likely to think or act — will be met with skepticism if the primary evidence offered is an appeal to authority (e.g., scripture, a great thinker, an ideology) or analysis that rests heavily on intuitions and personal experiences. Not only might such a theologian be regarded as a trespasser in the domain of psychological science, but a trespasser who isn't respecting local wisdom.

Psych scientists have good reasons for their skepticism and resulting methodological propensities, but that

39 Although it might never be eliminated in the context of an individual psych scientist or research lab, part of why psych scientists find their method to be trustworthy is the public, democratic, and cumulative nature of the scientific enterprise where bias is called out in peer-review or other public, often published, forums for reconciliation and debate. This is especially true with moves toward more scientific transparency as a result of the so-called replication crisis.

does not mean there aren't fair criticisms of this intellectual disposition. One consequence of having such a high evidential bar is slow movement from findings to theories that generate applied research and finally yield real-world applications. For instance, it would generally take a long time for a finding considering how children learn to think about God to yield a well-vetted application to religious education.

Other Characteristics of Psychological Scientists

Because most psych scientists identify as psychologists and the academy has grouped psychology as a single discipline, it is easier to characterize psychologists as a whole than psychological scientists in particular.[40] Nonetheless, what can be said about academic psychology, at least, is a good first approximation of what to expect of psych scientists more specifically.

Very collaborative

Theologians or other scholars coming from the humanities disciplines are likely to notice right away that psychologists are very collaborative. They commonly co-author journal articles together, sometimes with teams of four or five authors. They form lab-groups or research centers together to share resources, co-train doctoral students, and give each other feedback and suggestions throughout the development, execution, and write-up of a study. Even relatively lone-wolf psych scientists will generally publish with their

40 Of course, all generalizations of such a broad field are likely to have many exceptions. For instance, Gina Linetti's claim that "Psychologists are just people who weren't smart enough to be psychics" is not universally applicable.

doctoral students. In these ways, psych scientists are much like other scientists.

Relatively egalitarian

Like other human beings, psychological scientists are subject to prestige bias[41] and will pay more attention to the work of those who are highly regarded or bask in the halo of a highly regarded institution, but even so, psychologists tend to be fairly egalitarian. Most psychology journals use a double-blind review process whereby the authors of manuscripts are unknown to the referees and vice versa. Degrees and titles are not typically included at the top of articles. Psychological science is big and broad enough that there isn't any way to conclusively say that this university or that one is simply the best. Rather, some universities may be regarded as particularly strong in one area of study of psychology and another university as strong in another area. It is nearly impossible for a university to be strong in every area of psych science, and so general prestige is hard to gauge. Though it isn't a bad strategy to pay more attention to psych science coming out of major research universities, the field leaders on particular topics may very well be based at less prestigious universities.[42]

Psych scientists also tend to eschew strong affiliation with prominent personalities in the discipline. Though some

---

41 Henrich, J., & Broesch, J. (2011). On the nature of cultural transmission networks: evidence from Fijian villages for adaptive learning biases. *Philosophical Transactions of the Royal Society B*, 366, 1139-1148. doi:10.1098/rstb.2010.0323

42 To take some topics that are of likely interests to many theologians, one of the top psychologists on forgiveness, Everett Worthington, was based at Virginia Commonwealth University. A go-to expert on religious coping? Kenneth Pargament at Bowling Green University. The leading researcher on disappointment and anger with God is Julie Exline at Case Western Reserve University. None of these universities, I suspect, would be on the top 40 list in the minds of most university-based academics.

psychological scientists will recognize that they are working within the tradition of a notable figure in the field, they seem to get almost as much delight in empirically challenging the findings of their heroes as in finding supportive evidence.

Increasingly more women than men

My first few academic conferences as a young psychological scientist were actually religion conferences. I noticed right away that women were greatly under-represented and beards and tweed were over-represented. And then I went to the Society for Research in Child Development conference. The difference was stunning. Not only was I, as a male, in the distinct minority of participants, the whole ethos of the meeting was different. In addition to serious scholarly conversations, people seemed more likely to talk about their families and personal life, there seemed to be less posturing and sizing each other up, and there was definitely less tweed. Conference presentations were more likely to be just that, conversational-style presentations, instead of pre-scripted papers simply read out. Whereas the prototypical theologian is male, the prototypical psychological scientist is female.

Mostly English-speaking

More so than in most other nations, psychology has become a very popular undergraduate degree in the United States and so a large number of academic posts in psychology have followed. Because of the oversized influence of the U.S. academic market, the result is that psych science is large and growing. Nevertheless, as a younger, less prestigious scientific area (and one confused with psychotherapy), it does not attract the government or corporate investment that many other sciences receive. As such, it is still under-developed outside of some of the wealthier European and Anglophone nations. Even with a great hunger for studies coming out of Africa, Asia, and Latin America, the preeminent scientific publications still under-represent scholars from these continents. Psych Science, then, is largely steered by interests in the developed world and especially the Anglophone world. English is the undisputed language of the field and it is hard to get noticed without publishing in English.

Some Tips for Reading Psychological Science

A common question for theologians to ask me when they have begun exploring how to infuse their theological scholarship with psychological science is how to separate the good, trustworthy psychological science from "pop psychology" or findings and theories that are highly controversial. In this section I attempt to answer this question and some related ones concerning how to read psychological science well as a theologian.

Use the Buddy System

Undoubtedly you will have to do a fair amount of reading on your own, but whenever possible, seek a guide who is more familiar with the literature. Having a psychological scientist colleague who is willing to help you identify the most promising science for your project will (typically) greatly ease your navigation of the various box canyons, mountain tops, and wide-open plains of this young and rugged science. Note, however, that unless psychological scientists are active in *scientific* research or teaching, they are unlikely to keep up-to-date with the latest findings and theoretical developments. And so, a newly minted Ph.D. out of a research university may be a better resource than, say, a nearing-retirement clinical psychologist who has not produced any scientific research or scholarship in several decades.[43]

Where should you look for a psych science buddy? I would consider faculty members at faith-based institutions that have a strong reputation for bringing theology and various disciplines together, whether or not they have post-graduate programs in psych science. You might also look for graduates of these sorts of institutions.[44] Another place to look is among the authors of such publications as *The Journal of Psychology and Christianity*, *The Journal of Psychology and Theology*, *Psychology of Religion and Spirituality*, *Theology and Science*, and *Zygon: Journal of Religion and Science*.

Where to Look for Content

When trying to find trustworthy psychological science, I recommend the following strategy for non-psych scientists.

43 There are exceptions to this generalization and, depending upon where licensed, clinical psychologists may be required continuing education that helps keep them current.

44 Acknowledging my own biases and experiences impact these examples, I have in mind places such as Azusa Pacific University, Biola University, Calvin University, Fuller Theological Seminary, George Fox University, Richmont Graduate University, Seattle Pacific University, Wheaton College, and Westmont College. I also know that there are psychologists with theological interests at places like Baylor, Notre Dame, and Wake Forest.

Start with textbooks

Undergraduate or graduate-level textbooks from reputable publishers — particularly those that have several editions under their belts — represent well-vetted summaries of many tried-and-true findings and theories from the field. The best textbooks to reference are up-to-date but rarely do textbooks include material that is hot-off-the-presses — which is a good thing! Fresh findings are unlikely to have been rigorously replicated and challenged by other researchers. Textbooks are beneficial for getting a general "lay-of-the-land" and their references section may point you to landmark studies, leading researchers, and helpful review articles. David Myers and C. Nathan DeWall's *Psychology* (12th or 13th editions), is an excellent general introduction with a scientific orientation.[45]

> **Other Resources**
> **by Erin Smith**
>
> Two excellent resources include: (1) NOBA (all free) modules. They have pre-fab books, but you can also peruse by topic. It may be easy to miss important things because it's a bit of a choose your own adventure, but it's a great resource. Written for use in psychology classes as OER. I've written a module for them and can speak to the process. The modules are also short and full of supplemental

45 Myers, D. G. & DeWall, C. N. (2021). *Psychology, 13th edition*. Worth Publishers. My citations here are from the 12th edition (2018).

> resources. https://nobaproject.com/ All the modules can be found under the browse tab.
>
> (2) Exploring Psychology and Christian Faith" (Baker,2014) is a text I use in my intro classes (with NOBA). It's organized to mirror a typical textbook and they do a great job with the science, while also wading into territories of biblical views of human nature. Might be an interesting exercise for a theologian hoping to go to that same place.

Review articles

Review articles in psychological science attempt to synthesize a number of separate empirical reports that have been published elsewhere on a particular research question or topic. Sometimes two or more alternative theoretical perspectives or interpretations of the body of work are pitted against each other in a review and the review tries to draw conclusions about which perspective is better supported by the evidence or where evidential gaps still exist. As such, reading review articles is a helpful way to get a deeper understanding of a specific literature fairly quickly, as well as identifying key researchers, research methods, theories, and findings on a particular topic. Some of these reviews include *meta-analysis*, a statistical technique for pooling the findings of numerous studies. For theologians, such reviews may help identify whether the body of psychological research in an area maps onto a theological question or concept of interest. For instance, how well does the psychological concept of "attachment" correspond to dimensions of a theological or philosophical treatment of "love"? In what ways do "executive functions" in psychological science bear upon theological treatments of "the will"?

Review articles range in length, methodological detail, degree of theoretical engagement, and quantitative technicality. *Trends in Cognitive Science* and *Psychological Science* are journals that offer strong short-format reviews. *Annual Review of Psychology*, *Psychological Bulletin*, and *Psychological Review* feature longer reviews.[46]

Empirical research articles

Because psychological science often uses terms that are borrowed from common discourse or adapted from philosophical treatments, it may seem as though an area of psych science research is studying the same thing as what a particular theologian has written about. For example, you might find a text-book claim that giving a group of people a salient common goal can make them more cooperative, but does this sense of "cooperation" bear enough relevant similarity to a theologian's discussion of what takes place

46 Note that popular magazines such as *The Atlantic* and *The New Yorker* sometimes run articles on psychological topics. Unless these are written by a guest writer who is an accomplished psychological scientist, I recommend only accepting what they have to say after checking out their sources. I don't mean to be unfair to science journalists – they have very difficult jobs and often do very well – but it is extremely difficult for non-specialists to accurately capture what research does and doesn't show. The same caution applies to popular science magazines such as *Psychology Today* (which psych scientists generally ignore entirely) and even *Scientific American* or *American Psychologist*, again, unless the articles are written by a reputable psychological scientist. In that case, these reviews can be very helpful entry points into a literature. Philosopher Christian Miller is an exception to these reading heuristics. He has written some very nice, appropriately qualified summaries of psychological studies related to various character strengths and virtues for popular magazines such as *Forbes*, but then he has written entire books on *Moral Psychology* (Cambridge, 2021), and *Honesty: The Philosophy and Psychology* of a *Neglected Virtue* (Oxford, 2021).

when one "cooperates" with the Holy Spirit? The devil is in the *operationalization* details— a topic I take up in the final chapter. Though some reviews will give enough details to determine how key concepts have been operationalized (i.e., represented in terms of specific operations for the sake of the study, including measures and procedures), it may be helpful to read primary-source empirical research articles for these details. There are many reputable, double-blind, peer-reviewed[47] psychological journals published by well-known presses and by professional associations such as the *American Psychological Association* and the *Association for Psychological Science*. I recommend empirical research articles in these disciplinary or subfield journals over general science publications.

Topical books

Unlike in theology, books are not held in particularly high esteem in psychology. It is not uncommon for a very accomplished psych scientist to never write one, and non-tenured faculty members are often actively discouraged from writing them. Books can be a great way to tell a bigger story or attract attention to a topic, but they are not regarded as the place one should (typically) turn for a rigorous and measured presentation of the facts of a study. In many cases, books are where psych scientists will allow themselves looser tethers to the basic findings and speculate a bit more boldly. As a result, though books can be helpful for seeing how a number of different lines of research might be

47 Most but not all psych science journals attempt to mask the identity of the authors from the reviewers and vice versa.

woven together, they carry some risks when relied on too heavily. When a book is published by a recognized expert in a topical space, however, books can offer accessible introductions to an area that is otherwise scattered over numerous incremental journal articles that only tell part of the story.

What to Look for

When exploring psychological science that might be useful to theologians, I recommend looking for…

- Scientific work that is not so recent that it does not yet have any published critiques or replications, especially replications from different research groups.
- Scientific work that is not so old that it is likely to have been superseded by more recent research; as a rough heuristic I recommend theologians privilege psych science scholarship between 10 and 30 years old.
- Topics that have been explored using multiple measures and methods.
- Research that has either used very large and broad samples or has been replicated across importantly different populations.[48]

48 In the humanities it has become common to try to include a diversity of author's perspectives (ethnicity, gender, etc.). In psych science it is more important to have a diversity of populations studied and research methodologies, particularly when considering particular findings or evidence. In principle, a well-conceived and carefully articulated psych science study will yield the same results when replicated by researchers of different national, socioeconomic, political, religious, ethnic, or other differences. But the same study may have very different results when it is conducted with populations that differ in important ways.

Some Key Terms, Concepts, and Values[49]

Various academic guilds gravitate toward common assumptions and language that may be perplexing to outsiders. When beginning to read psychological science, it may be helpful for theologians to understand a few key ideas and emphases that are broadly recurrent. Not only might these ideas be helpful for understanding psych science, but perhaps there are even some institutionalized intellectual virtues here that could be useful to theological inquiry.[50]

Perhaps the most preeminent value that distinguishes psychological science from some areas of professional psychology and from much work in the humanities is the relatively narrow way in which *evidence* is construed in psychological science. Like other natural and medical sciences, appeals to the history of a claim, how the claim is situated in a worldview or ideology, or to the authority of particular luminaries is relatively rare in constructing an argument in psychological science. Rather, the focus is strongly on observable, measurable, behavioral evidence. If you don't have such empirical evidence, you won't get much of a hearing in psych science.

As narrow as this may seem at first blush, what counts as "behavioral evidence" is broad. Anything a human or biological part of a human does could count. So, verbal responses to interview questions or surveys are behavioral responses, but so is breathing rate, eye-pupil dilation, amount of a particular food consumed in a week, or walking

49 See also Myers & DeWall (2018), Chapter 1, and the video *The Crash Course: Psychology, episode 2:* https://thecrashcourse.com/courses/psychology.

50 For more on reasoning and research strategies in psych science consider Erin Smith's piece at https://nobaproject.com/modules/thinking-like-a-psychological-scientist.

through a marketplace. Blood flow to parts of the brain or the firing of a single neuron could count as observable behavioral evidence in psych science.

These sorts of evidence are used to test *hypotheses*. Hypotheses are not just guesses or suppositions, but are empirically tractable claims, typically inspired by a theory or by observations.[51] As a school teacher, I might notice that the children in my class seem to do poorer on exercises the longer it has been since they have eaten. That might lead me to generate the hypothesis that children's blood sugar levels are related to outcomes on, say, math quizzes. Or, reading about Abraham Maslow's hierarchy of needs theory, I might extrapolate that children focused on a basic need such as food, have less capacity to invest in mathematical learning and performance. And so, based upon the theory, I generate a hypothesis. Both observations and theories may generate hypotheses.

Hypotheses are often conceptualized in terms of a null hypothesis and an alternative hypothesis, and are informed by how key concepts are *operationalized.* To illustrate, in one of my studies,[52] our research question was whether three- to six-year-old children can distinguish between the sort of mind that God has and the kind that a human has. But posing that question as a claim, e.g., "yes, they can", isn't a properly formed hypothesis. Rather, a hypothesis is more specific.

---

51 Occasionally the word "hypothesis" is also used to mean something slightly broader than a specific empirical prediction to mean what might be expected in variants on the theme as well. This sense of "hypothesis" may have some explanatory features baked in and so drifts toward a narrow "theory."

52 Barrett, J. L., Richert, R.A., & Driesenga, A. (2001). God's beliefs versus Mom's: The development of natural and non-natural agent concepts. *Child Development*, 72(1), 50-65.

Children's "understanding" of human and God's minds was operationalized in this study as children's performance on a well-used developmental task, a *surprising contents false-belief task*. This task has been used numerous times to gauge whether children's understanding of minds ("theory of mind" or "mentalizing" ability) includes the idea that beliefs may be false. Children are shown that a familiar container (e.g., a cracker box) does not contain crackers but something surprising (e.g., rocks). Children are then asked whether another minded being would be, like they were, surprised to find the unexpected objects in the familiar container. And so, "understanding others minds" was operationalized as performance on a false-belief task. The *null hypothesis*, then, was that three- to six-year-old children would answer the same for their mother or for God. The *alternative hypothesis* was that children would answer differently depending upon which being was asked about. Notice that the null hypothesis is a claim of no difference and the alternative hypothesis is the logical opposite. Psych scientists begin with the assumption that the null hypothesis is true. Hence, if the results are such that they would be very unlikely given that the null hypothesis is true in the world, the researcher *rejects* the null hypothesis. Consequently, the alternative hypothesis is *supported* (not proven!). In the case of this particular study, we found that five- and six-year-old children, on average, did treat God and their mothers differently in this task, recognizing that God would know what was in the box, but their mother would have a false belief about the contents. That is, we had sufficient evidence to reject the null hypothesis. Our interpretation, then, is that at least some children, at least in this domain, are able (at least under some conditions) to distinguish between the mind of God and the mind of a human being.

Psych scientists talk about operationalizations, null hypotheses and whether they are rejected, and alternative hypotheses and whether they are supported. You will also find psych scientists talking about *effects* and *effect sizes*. *Effects* are simply patterns of results, what typically happens. But usually the word is reserved for a pattern of results that leads to rejecting a null hypothesis. For instance, in an experiment — say, a study looking to see if consuming coffee changes speed on simple arithmetic problems — you might read that there was "an effect of condition," meaning that whether participants were in the coffee-drinking condition versus a non-coffee-drinking *control condition* was associated with a different pattern of results. Perhaps drinking coffee led to significantly faster responses and so there was an effect of drinking coffee. Likewise, you might read that in a particular study there was "no effect of nationality" or "no age effect," meaning that no statistically significant difference in the pattern of results among different nationalities or ages in the study. Note that *statistically significant*, here, means that the effect is great enough in magnitude to reject the null hypothesis; that this pattern of results (effect) is very unlikely to have come about by chance if the null hypothesis is actually true.

Effect sizes are measures that often supplement hypothesis testing. The rationale here is that a supported hypothesis, by itself, may tell little about how important the finding is. It may turn out, for instance, that there is a statistically reliable difference in effectiveness between drug A and drug B, but is the difference in potency big enough to justify drug B's much greater cost? Effect sizes help judge practical significance: whether a finding is something to get excited about. Just because an effect is (statistically) "significant" doesn't entail that it is meaningful.

When a pattern of results becomes well-established, that particular pattern may get named. For instance, recall the Garcia Effect: the common finding that getting sick to one's stomach a few hours after eating something will often lead to an aversion to that food (even if it wasn't the food that made you sick). The tendency for people to, on average, rate themselves as above average on almost anything — friendliness, car-driving skill, ability as a professor (!) — is sometimes referred to as the Lake Wobegon Effect, after Garrison Keillor's fictitious town "Where the women are strong, the men are good looking, and all the children are above average."

Once an effect appears reliable and replicable, psych scientists may begin to theorize about the effect. In psych science, a *theory* is a causal explanation of some effect or many similar effects. That is, a theory builds upon findings (effects) that are patterns of observable, behavioral evidence, but then extends beyond the known observations and effects. A good theory puts the pieces together in a plausible account about what generally happens in the mental or behavioral life of some specified population of people under certain specified conditions.

Although the early days of psychology were littered with grand theories to explain and connect wide swaths of human behavior, modern theories tend to be narrower in scope. For example, although Jean Piaget is recognized as a key figure in the development of studying childhood cognition, modern theories of cognitive development are more akin to "mini-theories," each tackling just a slice of the landscape that Piaget covered. Another example is Erik Erikson's lifespan development theory which has spawned a number of smaller, more discrete theories within each of his originally proposed stages (e.g., Marcia's theory of identity development). A strong theory—even a mini theory—generates new hypotheses for further empirical testing of that theory. And so, observations generate hypotheses which, when tested, generate effects, which inspire theories, which generate new hypotheses. Importantly, theories are not merely an interpretive frame or perspective, but are anchored by some collection of findings. Modifications or replacements of a theory must do a better job accounting for the same data.

The Structure of Empirical Papers[53]

Psychological research papers have a standard organizational structure. Once you know this organization, the papers are easy to navigate quickly, a handy feature if you are trying to read and digest a large number of empirical reports. The four main sections are the Introduction, Method, Results, and Discussion. I think of the organization as something like an hourglass.

53 Examples of this structure can be found in most articles published in an American Psychological Association journal. For more detail, see also the *Publication Manual of the American Psychological Association (7th Edition)*: https://apastyle.apa.org/products/publication-manual-7th-edition.

Introduction

Beginning at the top, the big, broad, research problem is introduced, often with examples of the real-world phenomenon that this particular problem addresses, some theoretical background, and a review of previous research on the topic. This is the Introduction. The introduction narrows as it proceeds, ending with a specific hypothesis or group of hypotheses that this particular paper is exploring. Usually one particular facet of a problem, one particular population, and/or one particular approach to the problem is the topic of the paper. In that sense, the paper goes from broad to narrow.

Method

The method section specifies what was done in this study with sufficient detail that another research team could, theoretically, replicate the study. The method section will typically describe the people who were studied and how they were recruited. Today this subsection is called "Participants" but it was previously (and more accurately but perhaps less respectfully) called the "Subjects" subsection. The "Materials" subsection specifies the tools used, including any materials used for measuring responses. Scales, inventories, and the like appear in this subsection. A "Design" subsection may specify the technical structure — the logic — of the method. A "Procedure" subsection provides the step-by-step sequence that the experimenter/researcher followed and what participants in the study experienced.

Results

The results section provides an analysis of the data generated by the study, typically with only very minimal interpretation. This section is still in the narrow part of the hourglass. If the study was quantitative, this is where statistical tests appear. The hypotheses specified at the end of the introduction and given detailed operationalization in the method section are reiterated here with their results. Were the null hypotheses rejected and the alternative hypotheses supported? Were findings statistically "significant"? What were the sizes of any detected effects?[54]

Discussion

The discussion section uses the results and material presented in the introduction to argue for a particular conclusion or interpretation of the data. Often the beginning of the discussion section includes a less statistically technical translation of the results before launching into the implications. This section is where the hourglass starts broadening again. What difference do the results of this study make on our understanding of the phenomenon under consideration? What questions has it left unanswered? In this section it is common for psych scientists to discuss alternative interpretations of the results and why they might favor one interpretation over another. Limitations of the particular study are commonly noted.

54 Traditionally, psych science follows a strategy of falsification. Criteria are established for falsifying a particular hypothesis. If the results of a study meet these criteria, the (null) hypothesis is rejected and its logical alternative (the alternative hypothesis) is said to be supported, but not 'proven'. An experienced psych scientist doesn't claim anything is "proven."

Research papers often include several studies in a single presentation. In these cases, this four-part organization may be made more complex but usually includes the same elements. For instance, a three-experiment study is likely to have a general introduction followed by a brief introduction to experiment 1, method, results, and then a preliminary discussion of experiment 1, which then motivates experiment 2. Experiment 2, then has a brief introduction, a method section, a results section, and then a discussion. The presentation of experiment 3 would follow a similar structure. At the end of the paper would be a general discussion with conclusions drawn from all three experiments.

I have found that knowing this general structure – introduction, method, results, discussion – is very helpful not only for quickly digesting empirical research reports, but also for generating a research proposal, even one that isn't scientific. The important difference, of course, is rather than having results to present, the "results" section foresees various possible outcomes of the proposed study and how these might be analyzed. Likewise, the discussion section of a proposal would describe how these possible results might bear on the research question and what questions would be left unanswered. Such an exercise often reveals weaknesses in the proposed research methods leading to helpful revisions.

THREE
Areas and Subdisciplines of Psychological Science

Psychological science is commonly introduced by presentation of its various subfields and I will follow this trend here. Note, however, that there is something artificial about these subfield boundaries and any given psych scientist may contribute to more than one. Some topics straddle these loose boundaries. Because these subfields are formed around topical foci, methodological orientations, and/or populations under consideration, the lines can be drawn a number of ways. I have tried to strike a balance between common convention and drawing attention to areas that might be of particular interest to theologians.

Biology of Minds & Behaviors[55]

Some psychological science primarily focuses on the biological substrates and mechanisms that are related to mental processes and behaviors. A guiding assumption is that for every sensation, thought, experience, memory, or action, there is a suite of biological (and chemical) states and processes that play a pivotal causal role. Biological psych scientists may wonder how the presence of a particular hormone impacts attitudes of a particular sort, the role that a specific brain structure plays in coordinating complex movements, how learning language changes a particular network of neurons, or how general physiological stress impacts memory formation. Scientists doing research of this sort may identify as physiological, biological, or neuropsychologists, but may also include a subset of neuroscientists (who study brains, neurons, and nervous systems), neurologists (who conduct medical study of neurological disorders), psychiatrists (physicians specializing on mental and behavioral disorders), and behavioral geneticists (who focus on how genes impact behavior) who apply their

---

55 For more see Myers & DeWall (2018), Chapter 2 and the videos at *The Crash Course: Psychology, episodes 3 & 4*: https://thecrashcourse.com/courses/psychology. For an introduction to the brain-mind connection with an eye toward theology, see Jeeves, M. & Brown, W. S. (2009). *Neuroscience, Psychology, and Religion: Illusions, Delusions, and Realities about Human Nature*. Templeton Press. Also consider Brown, W. S. & Strawn, B. D. (2012). *The Physical Nature of the Christian Life: Neuroscience, Psychology, and the Church.* Cambridge University Press. Full disclosure: whereas I agree with much of the advice that Brown and Strawn offer pertaining to practical ecclesiology, I am not persuaded that such implications only follow from an embrace of some kind of physicalism. Though written primarily for psychology students to understand how a Christian perspective may bear upon their research and practice as psychologists, it may be helpful to consider how neuropsychologist Paul Moes and cognitive/developmental psychologist Donald Tellinghuisen conceptualize the nexus of theology and psych science, particularly in their three chapters concerning biology. Moes, P. & Tellinghuisen, D. J. (2014). *Exploring Psychology and Christian Faith: An Introductory Guide*. Baker.

science to understanding human thought and action.[56] What unifies these various projects is an attempt to better understand human minds and behaviors through considering the biological substrate.

This biological study of minds and behaviors typically operates under a physicalist assumption, that all mental states and activities are caused by physical, biological mechanisms and can be fruitfully studied as such. What may be a useful methodological assumption, however, has become a widespread metaphysical assumption: minds are what brains in bodies do and nothing more. Successes of biological, especially neuroscientific, studies of minds and behaviors is widely taken by these scientists as decisive evidence against any mind-body dualism, or other position that rejects a physical monism, even if these scientists have not explicitly considered philosophical arguments on this topic.[57]

Nonetheless, it is not uncommon for psychological scientists of this sort to recognize that human psychology can be helpfully thought of as subject to both "bottom-up" and

---

56 Not all of these biological scientists are psychological scientists. One could study neurons, neurotransmitters, and brains for their own sake, just as one could study skin tissue simply to understand it better on the biological or biochemical level. Neuroscientists (for example) and psychological scientists are only partially overlapping sets.

57 The underlying framework is that we are biological machines that run on algorithms that can be discovered (eventually). An operational conviction common to scientists is that if we ever find something that appears to be a limit (e.g., "the hard problem of consciousness") that it's just a temporary limit because due to available technology and not a genuine limit to scientific discovery. For this reason, monism is easier for scientists to adopt; dualism would imply a genuine, irksome limitation of psychological science. I thank Erin Smith for this observation.

"top-down" causal influences.[58] Our biology impacts our thought but our thinking can also have important impacts on our biology. So called top-down causation is easily demonstrated. If you decide to raise your left hand, seemingly your mental decision causally impacts a cascade of biological events culminating in your raised hand. More subtly, your decision to read (and continue reading) this book is changing the strength of neural connections in your brain. Perhaps more interesting are the powerful demonstrations that human will is restricted by many sorts of biological influences, some of which we are commonly unaware.[59] This general theme, that there are processes of which we are not conscious that impinge upon our conscious thought is a recurrent one across many areas of the psychological sciences as will become evident in subsequent sections.

The phenomenal unity that we experience may be the product of multiple agencies or selves within us that — usually — work together seamlessly. The most dramatic demonstration of this possibility comes from the study of "split-brain" patients, people who have undergone surgical severing of the corpus callosum. The corpus callosum is a thick band of neural tissue that connects the left and

---

58 A view meant to capture these dynamics while embracing physicalism is termed non-reductive physicalism. See Jeeves and Brown (2009), Chapter 8. For a discussion of the embodied mind that sees dualism as feasible, consider philosophical theologian Aku Visala's, "*Imago Dei*, Dualism, and Evolution: A Philosophical Defense of the Structural Image of God," Zygon Special Edition on Human Nature as *Imago Dei* 49:1 (2014): 101–20. Psychologist and theologian Fraser Watts also sees limitations on how strong commitments to the mind as body has for understanding the self: Fraser Watts, "Embodied Cognition and Religion," *Zygon* Special Edition on Religion and Embodied Cognition 48:3 (2013): 745–58. Thanks to Erin Kidd for bringing these citations to my attention.

59 For a discussion, consider this collaboration by philosophical theologian Nancey Murphy and neuropsychologist Warren Brown: Murphy, N. & Brown, W. S. (2007). *Did My Neurons Make Me Do It? Philosophical and Neurobiological Perspectives on Moral Responsibility and Free Will*. Oxford University Press.

right hemispheres of the brain, facilitating the integration across these two, asymmetrical structures. In rare cases, to prevent severe epileptic seizures, neurosurgeons cut the corpus callosum. The result is a "split-brain."[60] Split brain patients have been very helpful in demonstrating how the two hemispheres have specialized functions. For example, much basic language processing takes place in the left hemisphere (in most people), and broader contextual and metaphorical thinking is (typically) subserved by the right hemisphere. The two hemispheres have functional redundancy as well but their specialization means that each hemisphere of the brain has a characteristic way of processing information — of thinking of and perceiving the world and reacting to it — such that it is as if we are two persons in one. A similar account could be offered concerning how our pre-frontal cortex, the evolutionarily new part of the brain that is in front of our ears and behind our foreheads, interacts in fascinating ways with our more ancient posterior and mid-brain structures. It seems that much of the conscious, deliberative, imaginative, and "rational" thought is the product of humans' distinctively large pre-frontal cortex, often overriding or reinterpreting signals from the older parts of the brain. Again, it is almost as if we have multiple selves that usually work harmoniously as a unity but injury, surgery, or careful experiments can give us glimpses into each of their characters.

---

60 An entertaining video introduction to "split-brain" patients featuring one of the world leaders in this research Michael Gazzaniga, can be found here: https://www.youtube.com/watch?v=82tIVcq6E7A. Naturally occurring "split-brains" also occasionally occur, a condition in which the corpus callosum does not properly form (agenesis of the corpus callosum). Warren Brown at Fuller Theological Seminary is a leading researcher of this condition.

Social Psychology[61]

Humans are fundamentally social animals. We aren't simply born into the world and left to fend for ourselves, but are born into family units and communities that share in our development and learning, which we, in turn, contribute to. Not surprisingly, then, a major subfield of psychology concerns the nature of our thought about others and how to interact with them, our identities as social beings, and how groups of humans form and engage each other. This subfield is social psychology.

What animates research in social psychology is a concern with the causes and consequences of human sociality. What are the factors that enable and motivate humans to be social, to affiliate with each other, to form families, cliques, friend-groups, and communities? How does group membership change how we think and behave?

A focus on the person as the unit of measure is what differentiates social psychology from neighboring studies of sociology and anthropology, even if the borders get a little fuzzy. Social psychology is interested in individual thinking and behavior, but social psychologists study individuals by exploring how individual relatedness and embeddedness in social relationships and contexts influence the individual (and, as a consequence, also the group). Importantly, a social psychologist studies the impact of the social world on individuals, whether that world is real (e.g., a person in a crowded location) or perceived (e.g., a person dancing

---

61 This section on social psychology was co-authored with Erin Smith. A great place to start for more information is Myers & DeWall (2018), Chapter 13, Biswas-Diener's *An Introduction to Social Psychology* on NOBA (http://noba.to/s64y5c2m) and also *The Crash Course: Psychology, episodes 12, 37, 38, 39,* and *40.* https://thecrashcourse.com/courses/psychology

alone in their living room, thinking about how everyone else, carried as a mental representation in their mind, would think their moves are awesome).

Social psychologists may focus on particular age-groups such as childhood or adolescence or take a developmental approach and so also identify as developmental psychologists (social developmentalists). Social psychologists may work in specific applied areas of research, such as how our best understanding of social dynamics might be harnessed to improve work environments. These social psychologists might, then, also be identified as industrial/organizational psychologists. A lot of social psychology is inspired by current social problems important to the psychologists, and so social psychology can readily find its way into popular discourse around these problems. Social psychologists may also focus on the thought processes that underly human social interaction, or what is called social cognition. Here, the introduction will focus on two important domains within social psychology: research on conformity and obedience and research on social cognition.

How are the Group Character Traits of Christian Churches Related to the Well-Being of Congregants?

T. Ryan Byerly has begun exploring this theological puzzle, he writes:

> How, for example, should collective character traits, in general, be conceptualized? What, more specifically, would make a collective character

trait of a Christian congregation a virtue or vice? And how might a congregation's possession of collective virtues or vices be related to various aspects of the well-being of congregants, such as their spiritual well-being, satisfaction with life, and satisfaction with their church?

Drawing upon philosophy, theology, and organizational psychology he seeks to make progress on these questions.

https://www.theo-puzzles.ac.uk/2021/06/05/trbyerly/

Conformity and Obedience

Social psychology has yielded many of psychological science's most memorable studies—perhaps they are memorable because they often demonstrate how much who we are relies upon our social context. Solomon Asch demonstrated that — at least under some conditions — adults will deny the veracity of their own senses if the consensus of the group is against them. Adults were asked to tell which of three lines was the longest, and though the correct answer was obvious (if the participants would have been alone), if the others in the room were consistent in answering incorrectly, about a third went along with the incorrect answer.[62] Working in the aftershock of Nazi atrocities, Stanley Milgram's infamous obedience studies vividly demonstrated how social roles, particularly when directed by those in authority positions, can prompt people to behave

62 Asch, S. E. (1955). Opinions and social pressure. *Scientific American*, 193, 31-35. See also: https://www.youtube.com/watch?v=iRh5qy09nNw The general pattern, that social conformity changes our actions, has been replicated directly and conceptually many times. This precise task (judging line lengths) yields different rates of conformity across cultures and even across time in individual societies.

in ways that importantly deviate from either their day-to-day selves or how they understand their true selves. In one trial, over 60 percent of adults who were assigned the role of "teachers" administering shocks to a "learner" (actually a "confederate" of the experimenter — the shocks weren't real), conformed with instructions to shock the learners with what they thought were dangerous electrical charges.[63]

Not only can social pressure breed conformity and social roles change attitudes and behaviors, but sometimes being part of a group also leads to disturbing inaction. *Bystander apathy* (or the *Bystander Effect*) is the term for those occasions in which being part of a group creates a diffusion of responsibility such that no one acts to address a wrong,[64] as when a child is struck by a car and dozens of onlookers fail to do anything to help.[65] It is as if people conform to the apathy of the group; everyone else's passivity suggests to me that it is someone else's problem or not a problem at all. Even if I perceive a problem, I may be looking to others for a cue as to what to do about it, a cue that doesn't come.

A greatly overblown, but famous, social psychological experiment was conducted with Princeton Seminary students. Known as the "Good Samaritan" study, seminary students were asked to prepare a short talk and then told

---

63 Milgram, S. (1963). Behavioral study of obedience. Journal of *Abnormal & Social Psychology*, 72, 207-217. The Khan Academy summarizes main takeaways from the Milgram studies here: https://www.youtube.com/watch?v=LTZKp8nOhVU.

64 Darley, J. M. & Latané, B. (1968). "Bystander intervention in emergencies: Diffusion of responsibility". *Journal of Personality and Social Psychology*. 8,(4, Pt.1), 377–383. doi:10.1037/h0025589. PMID 5645600. Latané, B. & Darley, J. M. (1968). "Group inhibition of bystander intervention in emergencies". *Journal of Personality and Social Psychology*. 10 (3), 308–324. doi:10.1037/h0026570. PMID 5704479. See also: https://www.youtube.com/watch?v=OSsPfbup0ac

65 https://en.wikipedia.org/wiki/Death_of_Wang_Yue

to walk to another location to deliver it, passing by a collapsed actor who pretended to be suffering from a health problem. Some students were randomly assigned to give their talk on the parable of the Good Samaritan, others to talk about various career options for seminary graduates. Seminarians were also randomly assigned to different conditions of hurry: some were given lots of time to walk to the location of their talk, others were gently hurried, and others were told to urgently rush to give their talk. The measure of interest? Did seminarians stop to help the collapsed and ill person? Seminarians who were hurried were much less likely to stop to help — a fairly stable finding in other populations and situations. When we are in a hurry, most of us are much less likely to help other people. Whether seminarians were asked to talk about the parable of the Good Samaritan did not lead to any statistically significant change in how much help the seminarians gave. Contrary to many popular treatments of this study, however, many Princeton seminarians did stop to help (40% of the 40 in the study), and though thinking about the Good Samaritan did not lead to a large enough difference among conditions to be statistically significant, it is erroneous to conclude that seminarians were not impacted by being reminded of the parable. Of those in the parable condition 53% stopped to help. In the career-options condition 29% stopped. The sample size was too small for this difference to register as statistically significant. No comparison with non-seminarians was included and so it could be that the helpfulness of seminarians was much greater or much weaker than comparable non-seminarians. The big takeaway, then, isn't that

Reformed seminarians are uncaring, but that social pressures – such as to hurry – can importantly impact our behavior.[66]

Who we are with can make us more or less outgoing, helpful, kind, aggressive, cooperative, or critical. Because of the many powerful demonstrations of how social factors apparently change individual thought and behavior, it is not uncommon for social psychologists to talk as if humans are mostly — or almost entirely — socially determined. That is, an individual is a product of their ever-changing social situation and there is very little self left to talk about. Such an interpretation goes well beyond the facts, but is influential nonetheless and it is worth considering: to what degree is a person individually responsible for their achievements and failures? Do the findings of social psychology impact how we should think about the praise- and blameworthiness of actions? Does awareness of the social factors that may be impacting our attitudes and actions free us to make better decisions?

Social Cognition

Research on social cognition, thinking about and thinking influenced by the social world, explores ideas around attributions and attitudes. Broadly, attributions are the way that we explain our own and others' behavior. Research consistently documents asymmetrical biases in our attributions. For example, we are generally forgiving of our own transgressions ("I *had* to cut that guy off on the freeway because

---

66 Darley, J. M., and Batson, C. D. (1973). "From Jerusalem to Jericho": A Study of Situational and Dispositional Variables in Helping Behavior. *Journal of Personality and Social Psychology*, 27, 100-108. The way that this study has been mishandled also serves as a reminder that psych science progresses mostly through lots of incremental studies that only specialists read and not, typically, through dramatic breakthrough studies.

I was going to miss my exit and there is no way I can be late for this meeting!"), appealing to situational constraints in our (less-than-great) actions (an illustration of the *self-serving bias*). Yet, when others behave badly, we tend to be less forgiving ("That *jerk* just cut me off on the freeway!"). When we explain other's problematic behavior by appealing to some internal characteristic (e.g., their "jerk-ness"), we have committed the *fundamental attribution error.* There are other asymmetries in our social evaluations, too, including the *holier-than-thou effect* (that we may not be the best, but we are probably "better than average" at levels that are statistically impossible) and the *just world hypothesis* (the belief that good things happen to good people and bad things to bad people).

Understanding biases in the attributions we give for our own and others' behavior is important because they can reveal, inform, and reinforce our attitudes, another important aspect of social cognition research.[67] Psych scientists understand attitudes to be our beliefs about and preferences for people, groups, ideas, etc. Research on attitudes, especially in the past few decades, has increasingly focused on issues of group identity and how group membership influences (or predicts) attitudes and behavior toward non-group members. Psych scientists refer to these groups as the in-group (either the majority group or the group that you are a member of) and the out-group (the minority group or those not in your group). Research on group processes yields strong support for the social (and groupish) nature

67 For a creative application to theological inquiry, consider: Zahl, S. (2021). Beyond the critique of soteriological individualism: Relationality and social cognition. *Modern Theology*, 37(2), 336-361. DOI:10.1111/moth.12686

of human beings, but there is active debate about how this plays out in the real world. For example, although there is documented preference for others in our in-group, this may not automatically entail the denigration of the out-group, though there are also clear examples of this kind of out-group denigration.[68]

Moreover, some popular methods of social psychology in areas of group biases and prejudice are not without controversy. For example, the Implicit Associations Test (IAT)[69] is a measure of group attitudes based on the understanding that long-term memory is organized semantically; items associated with one another are more easily recalled than items that are not closely associated. We would expect that after being shown a picture of a doctor, more people than would be expected by chance would complete the word stem "__urse" with *n*urse rather than *p*urse or *c*urse or *b*urse or some other -urse word. This is because exposure to *doctor* activates the semantically associated concept of nurse, priming that response. The IAT takes the same logic and examines the speed with which we sort positive and

68 Susan Fiske, who is well known in this field, has written an easy and brief introduction to stereotypes, prejudice, and discrimination, three constructs at the core of this kind of in-group/out-grouping. http://noba.to/jfkx7nrd Fu and colleagues (2012) discuss how in-group bias may have evolved (see https://www.nature.com/articles/srep00460) and Aboud (2003) explores the complicated relationship between in-group favoritism and out-group prejudice developmentally (see https://psycnet.apa.org/record/2002-11235-006).

69 You can take an IAT test to explore how it works here: https://implicit.harvard.edu/implicit/ Mahzarin Banaji describes implicit measures and the IAT in this interview: https://www.youtube.com/watch?v=ABSeKU2qJoI. Note that, strictly speaking, the IAT is a measure of association between two conceptual constructs and not a measure of prejudice or bias commonly understood. The IAT also requires participants to construct and use a concept or category that may not be normally used by the participants. For instance, age and race groupings are not the same in all people but the IAT, in effect, trains up participants in specific age- or race-based groups and then tests semantic associates of those ad hoc groupings. For these reasons, interpreting performance on these tasks – especially for any given individual (in contrast with large group trends) – should be done with care.

negative words when paired with different groups (i.e., black or white faces; young or old faces). The idea is that systematically faster responses is a demonstration of an automatic, implicit association of some human features (e.g., age, sex, race) and some other attributes (e.g., careers, academic preferences, goodness). There is evidence that these associations sometimes have real-world consequences, though how to interpret this evidence is subject to ongoing debate, especially as related to the practical import of sometimes very small effect sizes.[70] Although research on social cognition generally, and biases, prejudice, and discrimination specifically, may be valuable to theological inquiry, this research should be engaged carefully, to ensure that the scope of the field, including the nuances and ongoing debates, are well understood.[71]

Across the domains of inquiry in social psychology, the particulars of how social factors sometimes powerfully shape individual thought, feeling, and action may be useful to theologians interested in ecclesiology and areas of practical theology concerning community worship, prayer, and repentance. For instance, because our experiences and interpretations of events are importantly mediated through

---

70 Two resources in the development and support for implicit measures of important constructs related to social cognition are Anthony G. Greenwald and Mahzarin R. Banaji, "Implicit Social Cognition: Attitudes, Self-Esteem, and Stereotypes," *Psychological Review* 102, no. 1 (1995): 4–27 and Anthony G. Greenwald and Mahzarin R. Banaji, "The Implicit Revolution: Reconceiving the Relation between Conscious and Unconscious," *American Psychologist* 72, no. 9 (2017): 861–71, https://doi.org/10.1037/amp0000238. A discussion of implicit bias research that includes citations of some of the research that debates the conclusions drawn from implicit cognition research can be found in Erin I. Smith, "The Role of Psychology in Advancing the Dialogue between Science and Christianity," *Perspectives on Science and Christian Faith* 72, no. 4 (2020): 204-221.

71 Recruiting a psych scientist tour guide may be especially useful in this terrain, but especially in socially controversial domains, it may be helpful to actively seek out multiple perspectives.

what we perceive to be the experiences and interpretations of others, how we experience worship is likely to be greatly impacted by our worshipping communities. Perhaps social psychology has something to offer theology of evangelism and missiology. After all, presentation of the Gospel is (typically) a social, interpersonal engagement. Psychological scientists have generated evidence concerning the features of people that make them more or less credible and attractive as sources for information.[72] More radically, the deeply social character of humans may support missiological perspectives that focus on social- or group-level changes in preparation for individual-level changes rather than the other way around. Many other, potential, applications in thinking about personhood in theological anthropology, Christian community, and formation are possible. Social psychology depicts a story of the intertwined nature of human thinking and behaving, even in the context of deeply held intuitions (cultural or other) about the independence of individual behavior.[73]

---

72 For instance, consider the social learning biases that Joseph Henrich and colleagues have documented. We seem inclined to imitate or learn from people we register as prestigious, skilled, and relevantly like ourselves, as well as those whom others are imitating. Henrich, J., & Broesch, J. (2011). On the nature of cultural transmission networks: evidence from Fijian villages for adaptive learning biases. *Philosophical Transactions of the Royal Society B*, 366, 1139-1148. doi:10.1098/rstb.2010.0323. Henrich, J., & McElreath, R. (2007). Dual inheritance theory: The evolution of human cultural capacities and cultural evolution. In R. Dunbar & L. Barrett (Ed.), *Oxford handbook of evolutionary psychology* (pp. 555-570). Oxford, UK: Oxford University Press.

73 Concerning how relationships play a strong role in spiritual (trans)formation, consider *Relational Spirituality: A Psychological-Theological Paradigm for Transformation* by psychologists Todd and Elizabeth Lewis Hall (2021, IVP Academic).

Personality Psychology[74]

Another subfield of psychological science concerns personality, those enduring features that make each of us unique individuals. What makes me me, across time and context? In some respects personality psychology is the flip-side of social psychology. A crude simplification is that social psychology emphasizes temporary states and personality psychology emphasizes enduring traits. I once was told by a personality psychologist at a major research university that personality psychology is everything "left over" from social psychology. But he also noted that personality psychologists have to be generalists. That is, the study of what makes people the unique persons that they are benefits from considering their biologies, developmental histories, thought patterns, emotions, motivations, social situations, and cultural contexts.

It is common to talk about personality as having several different levels. These levels vary in terms of how context-independent or generalizable they are. For instance, very generally, we may say that some people have an easy-going temperament whereas others are more intense. This temperament is thought to be broadly generalizable across situations. But we know that not everyone who is "easy-going" is the same. There has to be more to personality than that. Dan McAdams has argued for three important levels of personality: dispositional traits, personal concerns (or characteristic adaptations), and narrative identity. Dispositional traits can be thought of who we are very generally, as a

74 See Myers & DeWall (2018), Chapter 14, and *The Crash Course: Psychology, episode 22*. https://thecrashcourse.com/courses/psychology. Erin Smith provided very helpful suggestions and text for this section.

stranger might characterize us after observing us across several settings. The personal concerns level tries to capture our key motivations and day-to-day goals or methods for navigating life. The third level, narrative identity, is how we think about all of the parts of our lives put together into a narrative that makes us who we are.[75]

One of the most thoroughly studied and widely used frameworks for measuring and thinking about trait-level personality is the Big 5 personality inventory, also known by the acronym OCEAN (or CANOE). The O stands for openness and refers to one's degree of positive orientation toward entertaining new ideas or engaging new experiences. Experientially or intellectually adventurous people would be high in openness. The C stands for conscientiousness, and means pretty much what the label says. A person high in conscientiousness is likely to take their responsibilities very seriously, be thoughtful of others, and try to perform tasks to a high level of excellence. The E in OCEAN stands for extraversion. Those high on extraversion are sociable, affectionate, and up for a good time. The A stands for one's degree of agreeableness, how much a person wants to help and please others and values getting along interpersonally. The N stands for neuroticism, but in this context does not

75 McAdams, D. P. (1995). What Do We Know When We Know a Person? *Journal of Personality*, 63, 365-396. https://www.sesp.northwestern.edu/docs/publications/557464623490a3fc35faeb.pdf. A theologically-minded person might wonder whether McAdams' answer to his title question would be the same if the person in question is God. Roberts, B. W. (2006). Personality Development and Organizational Behavior. *Research in Organizational Behavior*, 27, 1-40, examines the layers of personality (e.g., traits, motives, narratives) in the context of a model for personality stability and change described with the acronym *ASTMA*. Importantly, in this model, personality change seems to be the exception (1 factor that influences personality change), not the rule (4 factors that influence and produce personality stability). The pdf is available here: https://chrisblattman.com/files/2015/01/1-s2.0-S0191308506270011-main.pdf

necessarily mean anything pathological. The neuroticism subscale is meant to capture the degree to which one is emotionally unstable, particularly concerning the ease with which one lapses into negative emotional states.

An important feature of personality theories (and their assessments) is that personality traits are conceptualized as an "individual difference" variable, which is a psychological way of saying we all have them in some degree—more or less. Rather than a personality trait being binary (or "bucketed")—I am extraverted OR introverted—personality traits are dimensional. Many popular, non-scientific "personality tests" create categories of personalities as discrete labels for personality "types." This sorting is inconsistent with the best data on personality. As such, the Big 5 inventory does not type someone into one or more categories but, rather, places one on five continua with a percentile score. For instance, instead of typing someone as an introvert versus an extravert, the Big 5 might give an extraversion score of 52nd percentile, meaning such a person is roughly average on extraversion (sometimes adjusted for age, gender, and cultural context). The Big 5 is a trait-level measure because it attends very little to particular contexts and is fairly stable over time. Once one's trait-level personality matures in young adulthood, it does not typically change much.[76]

Though it may be more fun to talk about being an otter instead of a lion or a Hufflepuff instead of a Slytherin, the Big 5 or other scientifically-vetted measures of trait

76 A great way to learn about personality psychology is to take and review your own results on a scientifically valid personality test. You can take one such Big-5 assessment here: https://www.personal.psu.edu/~j5j/IPIP/ (the short version will work fine). The results will give you a percentile ranking for each of the big 5 traits, as well as a few of the sub-facets that make up that trait. Your percentile is generated by comparing your pattern of responding to other individuals in your gender and age group.

personality have more reliable utility for theologians.[77] A body of research shows that religiously committed people (mostly Christians in Europe and North America in these studies) are higher than the general population in Agreeableness and Conscientiousness.[78] Is this finding good, bad, or indifferent from a theological perspective? What if, indeed, a non-trivial percentage of any population are less able to enjoy social immersion and less likely to experience emotional highs — that is, they are very low on extraversion? How might this fact impact prescriptive claims about lived spirituality or practical considerations concerning guided worship? Will the (likely) majority of a congregation who are high on extraversion be as enthusiastic about all of the quiet alone time planned by the introverted leadership team of the church retreat or will they regard it as torture?

Less well-known are studies of personality on the level of day-to-day goals or personal concerns, the second of McAdams' levels of personality. Personality psychologist Robert Emmons, best known for his work on gratitude, termed these goals that characterize our day-to-day efforts as *strivings*. A way to discover one's strivings is to try to answer the sentence, "On any given day, I try to…." Examples might include, "…be a good friend," "…do my work with excellence," or "…please God." Emmons has found that, with some time and careful thought, people can usually generate about 10 to 15 of these strivings. These strivings can then be coded for how much they conflict with

77 On why you should stay clear of the Enneagram, see Sarah Schnitker, Jay Mendenwaldt, and Lizz Davis' article here: https://www.christianitytoday.com/ct/2021/january-february/enneagram-personality-psychology-research-based.html

78 Vassilis, S. (2002). Religion and the five factors of personality: a meta-analytic review. *Personality & Individual Differences*, 32, 15-25. doi: 10.1016/50191-8869(00)00233-6

or facilitate each other. For instance, it may be challenging for a college student to "try to have a rich social life" and "try to get good grades," at the same time. Emmons found that when one's collections of strivings generally support each other, that condition is associated with wellbeing.[79] He also found that "spiritual" strivings — for instance, those that reference God or religious themes — were associated with less conflict among strivings. It is as if strivings motivated by one's relationship with God can help reduce the conflict within one's overall set of day-to-day goals and, in this way, contribute to wellbeing. Emmons, collaborators, and I used this insight in a study of high school students participating in a Young Life service camp working in orphanages in Bulgaria. Students who came into the camp week with more conflict among their strivings were more likely at the end of the week to "make a decision for Christ."[80]

A newer area of personality research that does not cleanly fit McAdams' three-level model but moves toward his notion of narrative identity, is the study of what have been termed "primal world beliefs" or "primals."[81] Primals are guiding beliefs about the world and one's self and future that appear to organize one's experiences, motivations, and actions. Primals seem to characterize the world. For instance, some people generally see the world as a safe place whereas others see it as basically dangerous;

---

79 Emmons, R. A. (2003). *The Psychology of Ultimate Concerns: Motivation and Spirituality in Personality*. Guildford.

80 Schnitker, S. A., Ratchford, J. L., Emmons, R. A., & Barrett, J. L. (2019). High goal conflict and low goal meaning are associated with an increased likelihood of subsequent religious transformations in adolescents. *Journal of Research in Personality*, 80, 38-42.

81 Clifton, et al. (2019). Primal world beliefs. *Psychological Assessment*, 31, 82-99. http://dx.doi.org/10.1037/pas0000639

some see the world as full of possibilities and opportunities, whereas others see it as limiting and imprisoning. These kinds of narratives seem to operate broadly, much like traits, but whether they are as stable as traits and how they relate to traits is not yet clear. The character, stability, coherence, and impact of these beliefs is a subject of on-going research. If it turns out that these primal world beliefs have broad impact on individual motivations and wellbeing as is being suggested, it may be helpful for theologians (or theologians working with psychologists) to begin considering primals in relation to sanctification, for instance. Can primals change and be part of being "transformed by the renewal of your mind"?

Across these various levels and dimensions of personality, an influential perspective that tries to split the difference between an emphasis on social situation and enduring traits is the *social-cognitive perspective* commonly attributed to Albert Bandura,[82] famous for his Bobo doll experiments of observational learning.[83] The essence of the social-cognitive perspective is that our behaviors, internal personal factors (such as thoughts, feelings, and traits), and environmental factors all interact. We act in ways that shape and even determine the environments in which we will find ourselves, which influences how we think, which causally impact the actions we are likely to choose, and those actions impact our attitudes, thoughts, and how we view ourselves, which impacts the social and physical environments that we find

82 Bandura, A. (2006). Toward a psychology of human agency. *Perspectives on Psychological Science*, 1, 164-180.

83 Bandura, A., Ross, D. & Ross, S. A. (1961). Transmission of aggression through imitation of aggressive models. *Journal of Abnormal and Social Psychology*, 63, 575-582. See also *The Crash Course: Psychology, episode 12*, "The Bobo Beatdown."

ourselves in. The details of such a perspective has potential implications for personal culpability regarding our beliefs, actions, and our personalities.

Personality psychology has the potential to raise numerous questions for a science-integrated theological anthropology. For instance, to what extent is our identity equivalent to our personality? Are some aspects of our personality more or less in need of restoration? What if some aspects of our personality are more or less a function of genetics, epigenetics, or other biological factors? Are some characteristics of a personality more Christlike? What does it mean for our identity when our personality has been importantly changed by drugs, injury, or another psychopathology?[84]

It seems that personality psychology, as well as many other areas of psych science have great promise to contribute to a theology of sanctification and spiritual formation. As Crisp, Porter, and Ten Elshof claim:

> But while interest in the nature of spiritual formation has resurfaced afresh in philosophy and theology, psychologists have been engaged in this discussion all along. It is the modern dis-integration of psychology, philosophy, and theology—understood as distinct disciplines—that is partly to blame for this situation.[85]

---

84 I thank Laird Edman for suggesting several of these questions.

85 Crisp, T. M., Porter, S. L., & Ten Elshof, G. A. (eds.) (2019). *Psychology and Spirtiual Formation in Dialogue: Moral and Spiritual Change in Christian Perspective.* Downers Grove, IL: IVP Academic. The quote is from the introduction, p. 2. This volume includes contributions from psychologists, theologians, and philosophers.

Cognitive Science & Cognitive Psychology[86]

Some psychological scientists primarily focus on the basic building blocks of thought. What are sensations, percepts, intuitions, impressions, concepts, and memories[87] and how are they formed? How do our minds assemble these building blocks to form broader patterns such as schemas and narratives? How are all of these used to make decisions and solve problems, learn, generate explanations, and make predictions? In essence, the science of cognition and perception concerns how humans process information.

Psychological scientists identifying with these sorts of questions and problems commonly call themselves cognitive psychologists but, especially for those who draw on insights from multiple disciplines, may call themselves cognitive scientists. Cognitive science has roots in philosophy (especially philosophy of mind), computer science (especially artificial intelligence), anthropology, linguistics, neuroscience, as well as cognitive psychology.

Note that here "cognitive psychology" is not closely related to "cognitive behavioral therapy" (CBT), an approach to clinical and counseling psychology. In CBT and other domains concerned with "cognition," the focus is much more on the content of thought ("cognitions") than the structure or processes that bring about thoughts of any sort. A cognitive behavioral therapist may want to help clients

---

86 See Myers & DeWall (2018), Chapters 6 - 11, and also *The Crash Course: Psychology, episodes 7, 8, 13-16*. For an introduction to cognitive science with an eye toward some religious and theological applications, see Barrett, J. L. (2011). *Cognitive Science, Religion, and Theology: From Human Minds to Divine Minds*. Templeton Press.

87 A creative discussion of liturgy in relation to memory is Joshua Cockayne and Gideon Slater's (2021) Feasts of Memory: Collective Remembering, Liturgical Time Travel and the Actualisation of the Past. *Modern Theology*, 37, 275-295.

change unhealthy patterns of thinking and so needs practical knowledge of how to change thought patterns, but is particularly concerned with some modes of thought over others (e.g., healthy/adaptive versus unhealthy/maladaptive). Cognitive psychologists are (typically) much more concerned with how a person thinks at all.

Cognitive science can make use of a broad range of evidence concerning mental states and information processing. Verbal responses in carefully designed tasks, eye movement, speed at responding to a stimulus (reaction time), and pointing could count. But because of its interdisciplinary character, cognitive scientists may also use linguistic databases and texts (nowadays often analyzed using computers in an effort to reduce error and unwanted biases), computer modeling, and brain scans (especially in cognitive neuroscience).

Perichoresis
by Christopher Woznicki

The concept of *perichoresis*—that is, "mutual indwelling" or "coinherence"—has been used since the patristic period to make sense of the mystery of core Christian commitments like the doctrine of the Trinity and the incarnation. Yet, despite its apparent usefulness, the concept remains metaphysically ambiguous. If theologians seek to do theology in a manner that is intellectually satisfying they should either abandon the notion that *perichoresis* explains something and simply state that *perichoresis* in the

Trinity and incarnation is a mystery or they should give some account of what *perichoresis is.* In my recent work I have suggested that an account of *perichoresis* that places an emphasis on the notion of sharing some aspect of the mental life deserves greater attention from theologians. To motivate this approach to perichoresis I have drawn from the field of cognitive psych. By drawing upon research on mirror neurons and mind reading I have been able to develop an analogy for perichoretic relationships that might characterize the doctrine of the Trinity and Christology. In essence, just like there might be a mutual indwelling or sharing of mental states between humans, we might be able to speak of a perichoretic relationship between the mental states of the persons of the Trinity or the human and divine mind of Christ.

Woznicki, C. (2020). Dancing around the Black Box: The Problem and Metaphysics of Perichoresis. *Philosophia Christi,* 22, 103–121.

Woznicki, C. (2020). Penal Substitution, Limited Atonement, and the Problem of Universalism in T. F. Torrance's Theology" *Criswell Theological Review,* 18.

Woznicki, C. (Forthcoming). *T. F. Torrance's Christological Anthropology: Discerning Humanity in Christ.* London: Routledge.

Fallibility of Human Cognition

Though some cognitive scientists study excellences of human thought such as intelligence, genius, skill mastery, and expertise, an enormous and growing literature also documents the frailty and fallibility of human cognition from perception to decision-making. The picture we get from these cognitive studies is a human mind that cannot possibly process all of the information around it and so it takes lots of short-cuts to get things "good enough." This serves us well,[88] but sometimes "good enough" gets us into trouble. This science has helped show when and how we can form vivid, confident memories that are error-prone or otherwise fallacious; how our visual perception of the world around us is patchy and heavily influenced by what it is we expect to see and what it is we are paying attention to; and how our reasoning and judgment strategies may result in various self- and group-serving biases – an important area of research for social psychologists as well.[89] We selectively remember things that affirm ourselves, we find it easy to find mistakes in our opponents' reasoning but have a hard time finding mistakes in our own, and we judge ourselves better than average in many domains and conditions — the self-serving bias.[90] Previously, I noted that some of these documented errors in reasoning have fortified the rationale for careful, systematic, and quantitative methods in psychological science. Psychological scientists are aware of human fallibility and aggressively try to protect their inquiry against such errors.

An important and open question that may interest theologians is the degree to which the imperfections of

---

88 Gigerenzer, G., & Todd, P. M. (1999). Fast and frugal heuristics: the adaptive toolbox. In G. Gigerenzer, P. M. Todd, & The ABC Research Group (eds.), *Simple heuristics that make us smart*, 3–34. Oxford University Press.

89 These social cognition distortions may also provide resources for understanding Christian (and other social groups') rejection or distortion of science. Consider Smith (2020): https://www.asa3.org/ASA/PSCF/2020/PSCF12-20dyn.html

90 Forsyth, D. (2007). Self-Serving Bias. *International Encyclopedia of the Social Sciences*. Machmillan Reference USA. https://facultystaff.richmond.edu/~dforsyth/pubs/forsyth2008selfserving.pdf

human cognition reflect ordinary creaturely limitations, particularly for the kind of animal humans are, or whether some of these imperfections reflect human brokenness or "structural sin." Which of these processing limitations and tendencies would Jesus have been subject to? Which will characterize resurrected humans in the new heavens and new earth?[91]

Dual-processing Models

A major theme of cognitive science — but one that appears throughout psychological science — is that human minds seem to have multiple 'levels' of processing, distinguished by the degree of conscious access to that information processing. Some thought has content and processes that are consciously available to us when we reflect on an argument or consider which way we need to rotate an object to make it fit in a particular space. Other thought has processes that operate with little or no conscious awareness even when we are aware of the content. For instance, upon walking in a room where some of your friends are sitting, you may suddenly form the accurate belief that two of them are angry with each other but you may not know how it is that you formed that belief. And then there is that type of mental processing that takes place without conscious experience of the processes involved or the content of the processing. This kind of processing may lead to sudden insights or solutions to problems that seemingly just "pop" into our heads in the shower or while washing dishes. Exactly what

91 Theologian Simeon Zahl considers how cognitive biases and psychological disorders might be part of the human sin condition in a way particularly apt for those who teach theology to suspicious undergraduates: https://mbird.com/theology/hiding-in-plain-sight-the-lost-doctrine-of-sin/.

the relationships are among these different types of mental processing are debated and may vary depending upon the particulars, but the broad differences are impressive enough to many psychological scientists that the idea of dual- or multi-level processing is currently a major theme in understanding how minds work.

Generally a distinction is made between two broad "systems": a fast, automatic, more emotional, and less consciously available "level" of processing, sometimes called System 1; and a slower, reflective, deliberate, less emotional level of processing (System 2). System 1 is roughly our feelings and intuitions; System 2 is our reasoning. But these two systems typically interact. System 2 operates on the percepts, impressions, feelings, and intuitions provided by System 1. System 1 may use heuristics and other shortcuts to make decisions and provide judgments that System 2 can consciously evaluate and reject or simply accept. Indeed, this idea of dual-processing or a multi-level mind has become most famous due to the ways in which System 1 dynamics often leads to erroneous decision-making.[92] I have applied dual-process thinking to an analysis of belief formation, particularly beliefs that might be deemed "religious" such as beliefs in gods.[93]

Psychological Science of Emotion[94]

Emotion and cognition are hard to disentangle. It isn't easy

92 Perhaps the leading contributor to this way of understanding the mind and its real-world consequences for decision-making is Nobel Laureate (with collaborator Amos Tversky) Daniel Kahneman. See Kahneman, D. (2013). *Thinking, Fast and Slow*. Farrar, Straus and Giroux. Another accessible treatment of similar principles is Malcolm Gladwell's *Blink* (2007).

93 Barrett, J. L. (2011).

94 See Myers & DeWall (2018), Chapter 12, and also *The Crash Course: Psychology, episodes 25 & 26*. https://thecrashcourse.com/courses/psychology

to talk about emotion without talking about cognition, and it isn't so obvious that many areas that have typically been considered "cognition" are really free of emotion or affect. As mentioned above, System 1 cognition can be emotional. Judgments are often made once the amount of evidence in favor of a position "feels right." Some theorists think of emotions (at least some of them) as broad, superordinate cognitive systems that activate lots of other systems for particular tasks. So, fear helps focus attention (cognition) and perception (more cognition) to get as much information about the potential threat as rapidly as possible (still more cognition) in order to ready the body for needed action. Emotion and cognition blur together in human experience. Nonetheless, traditionally emotion is studied by different scholars than those who study cognition, and its connection with other psychological topics such as stress, health, coping, and mood disorders motivates me to give it its own section.

Scientists who study emotion disagree about the precise number of emotions that form the core of our emotional experiences and the degree to which they are universal in humanity. At least five basic emotions make essentially every list: anger, happiness, sadness, fear, and disgust. Surprise is a strong contender for a sixth. These emotions are expressed and recognized similarly around the world from infancy. Of course, most of us are aware of many more, sometimes subtly different emotional states such as contempt, guilt, shame, suspicion, and amusement. It seems that a challenge in pinning down what count as proper emotions versus states that have affective components (what about curiosity, envy, lust, love, and gratitude?) is the difficulty with complexity of how emotions are generated at all.

Various models of emotions are entertained and studied, applied, and refined by psychological sciences such as the James-Lange, Cannon-Bard, and Schacter-Singer two-factor models.[95] What all have in common is a role for triggering stimuli in the environment, some kind of physiological arousal state, and cognitive attributions or labels for the feeling. Do stimuli in the environment (e.g., a spider) trigger physiological rush or feeling (e.g.., increased heart rate and breathing, dilated pupils) that higher-order systems then try to label ("Fear!"), or is the sequence different? How important are the social cues in either triggering or labeling the feeling?

What is clear is that because our general physiological states change slower than thoughts can change, and sometimes slower than environmental cues, we can make many different attributions to the same underlying feelings or even find our experienced emotions bleeding into each other. Consider a surprise party. The physiological rush of surprise can quickly turn to intense happiness, fear, or anger depending upon whether the surprise was welcome and what comes next. And so, from a psychological perspective, it would not be surprising for activities that generate physiological arousal—such as crowded conditions, low lighting, loud music, dancing and movement—to be associated with

95 For a quick synopsis of these historically important accounts of emotion and citations to many of the seminal studies, see https://en.m.wikiversity.org/wiki/Motivation_and_emotion/Textbook/Emotion/Theories/Cognitive

amplified religious feelings and experiences as well, especially if the social cues are appropriate.[96]

Cognitive Appraisal in Emotion and the Doctrine of Forensic Justification

A stronger handle on how emotions arise and can be transformed or manipulated may bear upon the ethics and resulting strategies around worship services and proselytizing. At a conference I once had a former worship leader share with me that he had labeled an effects pedal for his electric guitar "Holy Spirit" because if he pressed the pedal and played power chords, he could get people to raise their hands in worship. I have seen firsthand how evangelistic youth camping programs may (inadvertently?) make teens more emotionally vulnerable through exhaustion. When are ministry programs removing barriers to people responding to the action of the Holy Spirit versus engaging in emotional manipulation? The better we understand emotional dynamics, the better we can answer that question.

96 Galen, L. (2017). Overlapping Mental Magisteria: Implications of Experimental Psychology for a Theory of Religious Belief as Misattribution. *Method & Theory in the Study of Religion*, 29, 1-47. doi: 10.1163/15700682-12341393.

> The scientific study of emotion may also give us unexpected insights relevant to a theology of joy,[97] the place in positive emotions in a theology of human thriving or flourishing, and even understanding which emotional states (if any) that God could experience. In what ways is God's anger or joy comparable to human anger or joy?

Psychological Science of Motivation[98]

In his letter to the Romans, chapter 7, it appears as though the apostle Paul shares a common human experience, the struggle between different drives within us. In verse 15, Paul writes, "I do not understand what I do. For what I want to do I do not do, but what I hate I do." (NIV). As Paul goes on to explain in this passage, this conflict within has important theological implications, but it also expresses a psychological puzzle. Why do we do what we do? Why do we fail to do things that we desire to do? What are the basic needs or rewards that drive people to act? What are factors or situations that sap our motivation or redirect our drives? The psychological science of motivation addresses these and many other questions of this sort. Motivation is hard to extract from its context and so, arguably, is not its

---

97 Recognizing this potential, Miroslav Volf led a planning project on the theology of joy that included psych scientists such as Robert Emmons and Pamela King as consultants. *The Journal of Positive Psychology*, Volume 15, issue 1 was dedicated to joy and included works that explicitly drew upon theology. The focal literature review was Matthew Kuan Johnson's (2020) Joy: a review of the literature and suggestions for future directions, *The Journal of Positive Psychology*, 15:1, 5-24, DOI: 10.1080/17439760.2019.1685581.

98 See Myers & DeWall (2018), Chapter 11, and *The Crash Course: Psychology, episodes 17 & 27.*

own subfield in psych science (at least not anymore), but it is important enough as a topic to give it its own space here.

When I was an undergraduate psychology student, the motivation course was one of only two on the curriculum that included working with rats in "Skinner boxes." That is, students learned how to use B. F. Skinner's operant conditioning techniques to shape the behaviors of rats. Why? Because at least one thread in the study of motivation is derived from the behaviorist school: we have drives toward certain actions because of a series of associations, rewards, and punishments that we have experienced repeatedly in our past. Some of the drives we have were built up so long ago and so incrementally, that we don't have any conscious memory concerning from where these drives came. From this perspective, someone might find herself wanting to wrap in a blanket and watch television when feeling down because, when she was a child, her mother would comfort her by watching TV. That pairing of TV watching with comfort was so thorough that now watching TV gives comfort.

Psych scientists concerned with motivation also consider whether some of our motivations find their origins in evolved complexes very much like instincts in other animals. Are some of our drives part of our evolutionary heritage because they helped our ancestors solve recurrent problems that they faced? For instance, as with the Garcia (cheeseburger) Effect, there may be very good evolutionary reasons for people to rapidly form aversions to foods that they consumed a few hours before becoming sick. Likewise, the fear or disgust that so many contemporary humans hold for snakes and spiders may be helpfully considered as part of ancient drives to keep us away from potentially dangerous animals.[99] Perhaps most (in)famously, evolutionary perspectives have been applied to address questions such as why it is that across cultures men are more sexually attracted to women younger than older than themselves and for women it is just the opposite (in general). If sexual attraction is primarily about seeking out the best reproductive opportunities (especially for men) and investment in children (especially for women), then an answer to this riddle is readily presented from an evolutionary perspective.[100]

More interestingly, the idea that there are content-specific emotional/motivational "engines" in people — as with other animals — because of evolutionary dynamics, has begun to be applied to "moral" judgments. Jonathan Haidt and colleagues' moral foundations theory is one such approach to normative reasoning.[101] The general notion is that much of our reasoning about what is good or bad, naughty or nice, is shaped by drives that are part of our evolved human heritage. These conceptual-affective complexes are culturally elaborated and specified but not entirely the product of enculturation. For instance, have

---

99 Öhman & Mineka (2001).

100 But this pattern may extend to homosexual attraction as well, which is not as easily accounted for by mating and child-investment strategies: Hayes, A. F. (1994). Age Preferences for Same- and Opposite-Sex Partners. *The Journal of Social Psychology,* 135, 125-133. This study cleverly uses personal ads as the dataset.

101 Graham, J., Haidt, J., Koleva, S., Motyl, M., Iyer, R., Wojcik, S. P., Ditto, P. H. (2013). Moral Foundations Theory: The Pragmatic Validity of Moral Pluralism. Advances in Experimental Social Psychology 47, 55-130. Graham, J., Nosek, B. A., Haidt, J., Iyer, R., Koleva, S., Ditto, P. H., (2011). Mapping the moral domain. Journal of personality and social psychology 101 (2), 366. But it is sometimes observed that making "moral" judgments and engaging in "moral" behaviors are not necessarily the same thing: see Purzycki et al. (2018). The cognitive and cultural foundations of moral behavior. *Evolution and Human Behavior*. doi: 10.1016/j.evolhumbehav.2018.04.004. And for considerations of how an evolutionary approach to moral thought might interact with an evolutionary approach to religious thought, consider Ryan McKay and Harvey Whitehouse's (2014) "Religion and Morality," *Psychology Bulletin*. http://dx.doi.org/10.1037/a0038455

you ever tried to serve cake to a bunch of four-year-olds? If any of the pieces are different sizes than the others, cries of "but it's not fair" will quickly fill the air. Haidt and other research teams have provided evidence that whether goods are distributed fairly is something we quite naturally develop intuitions about regardless of cultural conditions. This "fairness foundation" then drives our thinking about norms in a particular space. Beyond fairness/cheating, other candidate foundations from Haidt and colleagues' work include care/harm (e.g., care for those in need, don't hurt others); respect/subversion (e.g., respect those in authority); loyalty/betrayal (e.g., be loyal to your people); and purity/degradation (e.g., do not defile sacred objects and places). If Haidt's picture, or something like it, is largely correct, is this evidential support for Paul's claims about universal knowledge of right and wrong in Romans 1? How much are these moral intuitions good guides versus misleading guides to right behavior in need of restoration?

These evolutionary perspectives concerning motives, drives, and morality may be treated as merely descriptive analyses concerning why we tend to do what we do, but have little to offer (at least directly) what we *should* do or not do. But perhaps the most famous model of motivations in psychology is much less shy about its prescriptive character (and perhaps a bit lighter in terms of scientific heft). Abraham Maslow's "hierarchy of needs" places our needs in a sequence; some needs must be satisfied before others will strongly motivate. And, in Maslow's view, wellbeing — a good life — is a process of moving up the hierarchy. The most basic drives are to meet physiological needs such as hunger and thirst. Once met, says Maslow, people will seek to feel safe, secure, and stable in their world. Feeling sated and moderately safe, the social needs of loving, being loved, and belonging become more prominent predictors of wellbeing.[102] Next are esteem needs — to feel competent, to achieve, and to be respected — followed by "self-actualization," to live up to our full potential as unique individuals.[103]

Though Maslow's hierarchy has some supportive evidence and has been very influential, the complexity of human motivations, the infusion of new physiological and evolutionary perspectives, and considerations of individual and cultural diversity have, it seems, discouraged motivation researchers from putting too much emphasis on overarching grand models like this one. Nevertheless, this area of psychological science has a lot to offer theological questions such as the one that started this section. Why do we do what we hate? How can our drives, motives, and attitudes be better harmonized with our explicit convictions concerning how we should live? Can motivational psychology assist practical models of sanctification?

Developmental Psychology[104]

In Mark 10:13-15, Jesus teaches that entering the Kingdom of God requires being like a child. Could developmental psychological science be a resource for understanding what

102 For a treatment on belonging as a more fundamental need see Baumeister, R. F. & Leary, M. R. (1995). The Need to Belong: Desire for Interpersonal Attachments as a Fundamental Human Motivation. *Psychological Bulletin*, 117(3), 497-529. doi: 10.1037/0033-2909.117.3.497

103 Maslow, A. H. (1971). *The farther reaches of human nature*. New York: Viking Press.

104 See also Myers & DeWall (2018), Chapter 5, and *The Crash Course: Psychology, episodes 18, 19,* and *20*. https://thecrashcourse.com/courses/psychology

being childlike in the requisite ways might be?[105] And could it be that running the race of life (1 Cor. 9:24) is a developmental concept that might be illuminated by insights from developmental science? Could a study of human development even help us better understand, as Paul Bloom has suggested, the origins of good and evil in human hearts?[106]

In a typical university setting developmental psychology is one of the major divisions or subfields of psychological science, but the label "developmental psychology" functionally captures at least two different meanings. Some people who identify as developmental psychologists (or more rarely, developmental scientists), focus on the thoughts and behavior of some particular human age-group such as infants, children, adolescents, or the elderly. You might hear such a scientist say that children need to be understood "in their own right." We may want to know how children acquire new skills and information to better teach them. We may want to better understand the motivations and emotions of adolescents to be more effective parents and friends to them. Naturally, developmental psychology could be a great resource for ministry directed at different age groups.[107]

But there is another sense of being a "developmental

---

105 Barrett, J. L. (2019). Give up childish ways or receive the Kingdom like a child? In T. Crisp, S. Porter, and G. Ten Elshof (eds.), *Psychology and Spirtiual Formation in Dialogue: Moral and Spiritual Change in Christian Perspective*, pp. 254-268. Downers Grove, IL: IVP Academic.

106 Though his book is written for a popular audience and its title is a bit sensational, Bloom is a very accomplished developmental psychologist as well as an engaging writer, and so this book can be a fun way to begin exploring how developmental psych science might enhance our understanding of moral thought. Bloom, P. (2013). *Just Babies: The Origins of Good and Evil.* Broadway Books.

107 For a recent example, consider: Crosby, R. G., Smith, E. I., Gage, J. & Blanchette, L. (2021). Trauma-informed children's ministry: A qualitative descriptive study. *Journal of Child and Adolescent Trauma.* Advance online publication. https://doi.org/10.1007/s40653-020-00334-w.

psychologist," and that is to use a developmental framework or methodology to better understand a particular psychological phenomenon. Such a developmental psychologist might study the development of empathy from infancy through adulthood, or the how long-term memory changes across the lifespan. Development, in this sense, includes how things (people, capacities, etc.) change and how they stay the same.

As my doctoral supervisor Frank Keil would say, sometimes you can get insights into the mature form of a thing through studying its development, insights that are hard to get any other way. I find that this is especially true of complex phenomena for which there are competing credible accounts of how multiple factors are required to bring them about. For instance, my former graduate school labmate, Linda Hermer-Vasquez, was interested in how people use visual information in the spaces around them to navigate and find objects in those spaces.[108] Do we rely more heavily on the geometry of spaces or on colors, images, and other distinctive identifiers? Using a developmental approach, Hermer-Vasquez was able to show that babies use the geometry of a room (i.e., its shape) before they can make use of, say, the color of a wall. Older children can integrate both types of information. This finding suggested the primacy of the layout or shape of space for navigation. Interestingly, Hermer-Vasquez also devised an experimental paradigm that overwhelmed the conscious attention of adults when trying to remember the location of

108 Hermer-Vasquez, L., Spelke, E. S., & Katsnelson, A. S. (1999). Sources of flexibility in human cognition: dual-task studies of space and language. *Cognitive Psychology*, 39, 3-36.

an object in a simple rectangular room. The result was that adults, too, lost the ability to reliably use wall color but they could still use the shape of the room to find the object. The adults performed like infants. Sometimes a developmental approach to a problem can carve a complex phenomenon at its psychological joints.[109] In many ways, developmental science is a lens by which questions in other areas of psychology (e.g., personality, social, cognitive) can be probed to advance understanding.

Developmental psychological scientists often identify either by a focal developmental age-group (e.g., a child developmentalist) or by a broad domain of concern (e.g., social developmentalist, cognitive developmentalist). It is not uncommon, however, for developmentalists to work across age-groups or broad topical areas because of the fluidity of some of these boundaries. A developmentalist concerned with language, for instance, may study first and subsequent language acquisition from infancy through adulthood, and may consider language from both cognitive and social perspectives.

Big Themes

A perennial big theme in developmental psychology has been the so-called "nature-nurture" debate. How much is a child's ability to take the perspective of another at a particular age, for instance, the result of natural, biological

109 A speculation inspired by Hermer-Vasquez's work and that by Daniel Levin and Daniel Simons' work on perception and attention for natural scenes: in worship settings that are cognitively taxing — as when engaged in verbal recitation and seeking to understand complex exposition — we might expect that the importance of physical layout of the space is more attended to than how it is decorated. Studies by Levin, Simons, and their collaborators are summarized in the book *The Invisible Gorilla: How Our Intuitions Deceive Us*, by Christopher Chabris and Daniel Simons (2011, Harmony).

programs versus a particular social or cultural environment? How much is a child's temperament the result of their genes versus early parental investment? But this "debate" is also perennially problematic. From conception, no development takes place independent of biology. Likewise, even before conception, a human is impacted by the decisions of its mother, such as her diet, activities, and so on. What she says can be heard by the developing baby in the womb leading to preferences for mom's voice and language at birth. And so, "nature" and "nurture" cannot be cleanly separated. Human nature is to be nurtured.

More helpfully, developmentalists have increased our descriptive precision of human development. Like other animals, humans acquire certain competencies in fairly regular sequences and at reasonably predictable ages. As a general rule, sitting up precedes walking, pointing comes before speaking, and social learning through imitation is obvious before deliberate attempts to establish a unique personal identity. These sorts of patterns have led developmentalists to wonder:

- How fixed or open are developmental schedules? And what accounts for any variability? Social environment? Genetic differences? Nutrition?
- How stage-like are they? Do we see spurts of development followed by plateaus or do we see something more continuous?
- How domain-general or domain-specific are these patterns of development? Does motor ability develop in a similar way as emotional

intelligence? Does thought about physical objects parallel how we develop in our thinking about animals or people?

Big Findings

The current state-of-the-art, at least by my lights, points toward humans having some more general learning mechanisms and some domain-specific learning mechanisms, each of which may have different developmental schedules. This complex picture does seem to have three big take-home messages, however.

Not a tabula rasa

Human minds are not, as many still suppose, blank slates (*tabula rasa*) that are passively written upon by their environments, or sponges that simply and indiscriminately "soak up" everything and anything in their environments. Rather, like other animals, humans are better at learning some things over others and play an active role in seeking out information that is relevant to the kind of organism that they are, in the typical environments in which they have typically found themselves. For instance, essentially from birth babies pay disproportionate attention to faces — they look for them, focus on them, and (sometimes) mimic them. Likewise, babies quickly form fear associations with snakes or snake-like forms and movement.[110] Sometimes called *preparedness*, these are just two well-documented

110 Öhman, A., & Mineka, S. (2001). Fears, phobias, and preparedness: Toward an evolved module of fear and fear learning. *Psychological Review*, 108(3), 483-522. https://doi.org/10.1037/0033-295X.108.3.483

examples of many ways in which human minds show selective eagerness to learn and think in some ways over others.

Impressive but declining plasticity

Whether we are considering cognition or brain physiology, babies are extremely "plastic" or flexible. Their brains readily form and re-form in reaction to their experiences. Babies' brains show the ability to reorganize and function well even after major brain damage or even the removal of large parts of the cortex.[111] This plasticity drops drastically through childhood and adolescence. Their openness to learning new things is, likewise, expansive and dynamic. Though they have natural predilections to learn some things over others, the range of possibilities remains enormous… initially. With each passing year, prior learning encourages new learning down some paths over others. For instance, in early childhood we can learn to distinguish among a very broad range of sounds, but once we carve up our auditory experiences, we begin to lose our discriminatory ability. And so, babies can hear differences in human speech that adults lose if those sound differences aren't used in their language environment. Though you can teach old human dogs new tricks, it is much easier to teach these tricks to *young* human dogs.

111 A particularly dramatic case study highlighting this plasticity is found here: Battro, A. M. (2001). *Half a Brain is Enough: The Story of Nico*. Cambridge University Press.

Sensitive periods[112]

It appears many domains of learning have sensitive periods, that is, phases during which learning is especially rapid, or periods that importantly set the table for future learning. Missing the learning opportunity during a sensitive period is hard to make up for later. Language learning is a textbook example.[113] For various reasons, such as greater sound discrimination abilities, language learning has a sensitive period in early childhood. Essentially, language exposure up to around age 6, has greater payoffs in terms of fluency than similar exposure post-puberty. Indeed, if children are not exposed to language before puberty, it is unlikely to develop properly ever. It is as if the language-learning circuitry becomes unavailable at a certain point. Use it or lose it. And language isn't the only domain with a sensitive period.

Another domain that shows early-life sensitivities is interpersonal attachment.[114]Originating with John Bowlby in the 1950s and 60s, attachment theory describes a broad range of ideas related to how people, starting in infancy, create and maintain affectional ties with others. Attachment itself is understood as both an emotional connection and a behavior regulation system. When an infant feels safe and secure with a consistent and responsive caregiver, the caregiver serves as a *secure base* for free (safe and secure) exploration in the world. Should the infant

---

112 Erin Smith co-wrote this section with me.

113 For instance, consider Norrman, G. & Bylund, E. (2016). The irreversibility of sensitive period effects in language development: evidence from second language acquisition in international adoptees. *Developmental Science*, 19, 513-520. doi: 10.1111/desc/12332

114 See *The Crash Course: Psychology, episode 19*. https://thecrashcourse.com/courses/psychology or Fraley's introduction to attachment across the life course (http://noba.to/s3kj9ufv)

experience distress, they can return to their caregiver as their *safe haven* for protection and the regulation of these anxiety-provoking emotions[115]. Research on attachment relationships highlight that humans develop a characteristic pattern of how we relate to others based upon early relationships — usually with parents. A secure attachment with parents sets a pattern for (typically) confident development of secure relationship with others later in life. Unpredictable interactions with parents, either because of parenting style or real instability in the world around, may prompt children to develop an anxious attachment style that they will carry with them in life. Such people may find themselves inclined to anxiously cling to others in relationships, out of fear of being abandoned. Babies who find their primary caregivers detached or unreliable may adopt an avoidant attachment style. Such people may have a life-long tendency to be mistrusting in relationships[116]. Interestingly, these relational styles may impact ones relationship to God, too. It may be

---

115 Although John Bowlby is credited with the initial formation of attachment theory, its specification as an empirical theory is indebted to Mary Ainsworth, the developer of the *strange situation* method, the classification system of attachment styles, and key language such as secure base and safe haven. Bowlby and Ainsworth's collaboration in the development of attachment theory is described by Inge Bretherton (1992). The Origins of Attachment Theory: John Bowlby and Mary Ainsworth. *Developmental Psychology*, 28(5), 759-775. doi: 10.1037/0012-1649.28.5.759

116 Hazen and Shaver (1987) were among the first to empirically connect adult romantic attachment with childhood attachment. Hazan, C., & Shaver, P. R. (1987). Romantic love conceptualized as an attachment process. *Journal of Personality and Social Psychology*, 52, 511-524. Today, there are a large number of measures for adult attachment to better understand how early attachment relationships shape and determine later attachments (friendships and romantic relationships). Like other "grand" theories in psychology, attachment is increasingly understood with mini-theories, each exploring specific components of and influences on attachment relationships and quality. As such, it is important to keep in mind the potential limits of attachment concepts, especially as proposed early in the theory development, as related to emerging and empirically nuanced assessments of these concepts.

that God satisfies a secure attachment figure for people who need one.[117]

Bowlby proposed that infant attachments to caregivers have life-long implications for future relationships because of the effects on internal working models (IWM). IWMs are a relatively stable (though not deterministic), internal template that we use to understand ourselves, others, and the proper relationship between ourselves and others. Although some research may still use the language of IWMs, similar ideas may masquerade in different language (e.g., implicit memory structures, cognitive schemas), grounding the concept closer to cognitive science than the psychodynamic roots of Bowbly's theory. Like other "grand" theories in psychology, attachment is increasingly understood with mini-theories, each exploring specific components of and influences on attachment relationships and quality. For example, the influence of attachment and the experience of social support on positive life outcomes explores one component of the broader attachment theory[118]. As with any thin slice, it is important to keep in mind the potential limits of attachment concepts, especially as proposed early in the

117 Schnitker, S. A., Porter, T. J., Emmons, R. A., and Barrett, J. L. (2012). Attachment Predicts Adolescent Conversions at Young Life Religious Summer Camps. *International Journal for the Psychology of Religion*, 22, 198-215. doi: 10.1080/10508619.2012.670024. See also the work of Lee A. Kirkpatrick and Pehr Granqvist on attachment to God.

118 For example, Feeney and Collins (2015) describe social support as a key component to thriving through an attachment lens. Feeney, B. C., & Collins, N. L. (2015). A New Look at Social Support: A Theoretical Perspective on Thriving Through Relationships. *Personality and Social Psychology Review,* 19(2), 113-147. doi: 10.1177/1088868314544222. Smith and Crosby (2021) use this social support background to experimentally (i.e., causally) examine how the introduction of socially supportive (i.e., attachment creating) practices in church children's ministry influence children's prosocial behavior. Smith, E. I. & Crosby, R. G. (2021). The Effect of Socially Supportive Church Ministry on Children's Prosocial Behavior: An Experimental Study of Latin American Protestant Congregations. *Journal of Prevention & Intervention in the Community* [Advance Online Publication]. https://doi.org/10.1080/10852352.2021.1924591.

theory development, as related to emerging and empirically nuanced assessments of these concepts.

A big takeaway from attachment research is that early learning in this particular domain colors its exercise throughout life, as with many other examples of "sensitive period" learning. Implications for parenting and education are manifold.

Humans are Mind Readers

One trait of being human that distinguishes us from other animals is the degree to which we constantly try to understand what each other are thinking and feeling. An important area of developmental psych science that falls on the border of cognitive and social development is the study of how people come to understand others as minded, intentional agents and not mere objects or living things that only respond contingently to environmental conditions. This area of research is variously termed *mindreading*, *theory of mind*, and *mentalizing*[119]and focally concerns how humans come to conceive of (typically in early childhood) mental states such as beliefs, desires, and emotions, and how they motivate action. Once we recognize that mental states guide each other's actions (as well as our own), we have the capacity for rich and complex social relations. When two people know that they are paying attention to the same thing – a capacity called *joint attention* – they can exchange information about it, and care about the thing together. Teaching

119 Not to be confused with philosophy of mind. *Theory of mind* is a term inspired by the idea that, like junior scientists, children form 'theories' about things around them that capture their experiences but go beyond them as well. Some theorists avoid this term because it carries these additional theoretical commitments.

and learning are facilitated. It may be, too, that the degree to which people can share in the attention and intentions of others is critical for making us the cultural species that we are. For these reasons, an enormous amount of research has concerned various aspects of mentalizing, when and how it develops in childhood, when it might not develop in a typical fashion (as in Autism Spectrum Disorders), and which aspects of mentalizing we see in other species.[120]

Does the Indwelling of the Holy Spirit require a Neurotypical Brain?
by Joanna Leidenhag

Recently, some theologians have been drawn to use developmental psychology and autism studies in particular to inform their understandings of what it means to be indwelt by the Holy Spirit. The basic idea is that indwelling describes a believer's ability to engage in joint attention with God to a maximal degree. Joint attention and Theory of Mind research have both been at the forefront of psychology research in autism. In my work, I explore whether this is a helpful way to use psychological science in theology by thinking through what such a project means for autistic Christians.

Does the Indwelling of the Holy Spirit Require a Neurotypical Brain? – Theological Puzzles (theo-puzzles.ac.uk)

---

120 Though it isn't an easy book, Michael Tomasello's *Becoming Human: A Theory of Ontogeny* (2019, Belknap) is a thoroughly empirically grounded argument for how human mentalizing develops and undergirds much of what makes humans distinctive.

Presumably considering the thoughts of divine beings is also informed and constrained by how our *mentalizing* capacities work. Thus, some psychologists of religion and cognitive scientists of religion have begun looking at how children mentalize with regard to ghosts, angels, and God.[121]

Psychological Health & Disorders[122]

The large majority of people who identify as psychologists specialize in some area of mental health.[123] On the scientific end of things, psychological science is put to action in trying to understand various mental, emotional, and behavioral ailments or disorders and what effective techniques might help people become healthier. Broadly, much of this area is known as *psychopathology*, but many negative psychological states and ailments aren't always as particularly enduring or abnormal as the term "psychopathology" may suggest. Clinical, counseling, and health psychologists work in this space among other health care professionals such as marriage and family therapists, clinical social workers, and psychiatrists.

121 Perhaps the easiest entry to this literature is my own *Born Believers: The Science of Children's Religious Belief* (2012, The Free Press), but research has moved on since then. Some developmental, cross-cultural cognitive science of religion appears in Hornbeck, R. G., Barrett, J. L. and Kang (Hernandez), M. (eds.) (2017). *Religious Cognition in China: Homo Religiosus and the Dragon*. Springer International. Practical theologian J. Bradley Wigger has also made important contributions in this space through his cross-cultural program of research concerning how children think about God in comparison to their imaginary friends: Wigger, J. B. (2019). *Invisible Companions: Encounters with Imaginary Friends, God, Ancestors, and Angels*. Stanford University Press.

122 See Myers & DeWall (2018), Chapters 12, 15, and 16. See also *The Crash Course: Psychology, episodes 26, 28-36.*

123 Essentially all faith-based doctoral psychology programs focus on areas related to mental and physical health and the bulk of efforts to integrate psychology and theology concern how to bring theological (mostly Christian) perspectives to bear on the study and practice of mental health. Examples of doctoral programs that are focused on this integration are those at Azusa Pacific University, Biola University/Rosemead, Fuller Theological Seminary, George Fox University, Regent University, and Wheaton College.

What Counts as "Disorder"?

Psychopathology concerns such questions as: What are the causes and most effective treatments for bipolar illness? Is schizophrenia a single family of disorders or several different disorder? Why do anxiety, depression, and other mood disorders seem to be on the rise in many societies? Psychopathology also wrestles with many thorny issues around what counts as pathology and what is mere statistical divergence from the typical. For this reason, this area of psychological science has much more explicit discussion of normative claims — what is healthy and good for individuals and societies — than many other areas of psychological science. Furthermore, what counts as 'pathology' is constantly under revision, and not just because of updates in the scientific state-of-the-art, but largely because of changes in societal values.

For instance, common diagnostic indicators of many psychological pathologies include whether the condition is distressing or socially disabling for the person who experiences the condition. And so, hypothetically, peculiar personal ritual cleansing that becomes socially accepted (e.g., as an expression of religious devotion), may no longer result in social exclusion or cause distress in the one who displays such fastidiousness. Thus, this behavioral routine may not rise to the level of "disorder" or "pathology" unless there were some other ill-effect (such as an ill effect on physical health). Examples of such diagnostic criteria — and how they have changed with time — can be found by inspecting various editions of the American Psychiatric Association's

Diagnostic and Statistical Manual (DSM), now in its fifth edition, which notably "takes a lifespan perspective recognizing the importance of age and development on the onset, manifestation, and treatment of mental disorders."[124]

A quick note of clarification: though clinical and counseling psychologists of various stripes use the American Psychiatric Association's DSM for diagnostic guidance, psychologists and psychiatrists follow importantly different educational pathways and have different qualifications. Psychiatrists have trained in medicine (with an M.D. as their terminal degree) and have specialized in the treatment of psychopathology, primarily through medical means such as the administration of medications. Clinical psychologists have much more focused training in psychopathology and other areas of psychology and have (typically) acquired substantial experience in psychological testing and therapeutic techniques on their way to their doctorate, which may be a Psy.D. (if the emphasis was professional/practical) or a Ph.D. (if there was more research/scholarly emphasis). Nonetheless, it is the American Psychiatric Association that, in the United States at least, is the primary body determining what counts as mental illness or psychopathology.

As suggested above, psych scientists concerned with mental health may also study less extreme and more common ways in which emotional states and mental processes may impact our health. The study of stress and how to cope with it, or dealing with grief and bouts of depression, are examples. Likewise, psych scientists have demonstrated that non-pathological (but enduring) levels of

124 https://www.ncbi.nlm.nih.gov/books/NBK519711/

anxiety can make us vulnerable for viral infections and other illnesses, or lead to dangerous ulcers. At many points, the lines between psychological or mental health and medical or physical health become invisible.

Mental health care professionals tend to understand psychological disorders as the net result of *vulnerabilities* and *current stressors.* Differences in individuals' genetics, developmental experiences including abuse or neglect, and cognitive patterns may predispose them to the experience of a psychological disorder. And yet, predispositions on their own are usually insufficient for the expression of a disorder. Thus, these vulnerabilities stack up, increasing the likelihood that a stressor will be capable of triggering the onset of the disorder. Two individuals with different predispositions can experience the same stressor for different outcomes.

Illustrative Disorders

As with many medical diagnoses, how to identify and categorize disorders has changed over time and will continue to do so. As with any efforts to identify what is "normal," "disordered," "pathological," and so on, such categorizations are not merely determined by the scientific facts of the matter, but also the values of the decision-makers as shaped by personal and social factors. Hence, this is a space in which intrepid philosophers and theologians could make a meaningful contribution, particularly when considering if and when people (individuals and communities) need help and what kind.

Anxiety-related disorders

Anxiety is increasingly receiving popular attention in many contemporary societies, so various anxiety-related disorders may be familiar such as generalized anxiety disorder, panic disorders of different flavors, phobias, obsessive-compulsive disorder (OCD), and post-traumatic stress disorder (PTSD).

Mood disorders

So-called mood disorders concern irregular or disabling states of sadness, irritability, or (more rarely) euphoria. These include many common depressive disorders such as major depressive disorder, seasonal affective disorder (in which mood is depressed when sunlight levels are low), and bipolar illness. Severe mood disorders and anxiety disorders can lead to self-harm and even suicide.

Schizophrenia

Variations of schizophrenia are characterized by hallucinations, distorted beliefs (delusions), diminished or inappropriate emotions, and/or disorganized speech. During a summer internship at a psychiatric research hospital, I met a woman suffering from schizophrenia who had the delusion that she was the Virgin Mary. Among patients who have delusions, thinking they are Jesus Christ are not uncommon. For these reasons, and because of auditory hallucinations (e.g., hearing voices), some scholars have leapt to the conclusion that there is some close relationship between schizophrenia and religions. Though it may be that, in some cultural conditions, a person who suffers from schizophrenia may be treated as having a demon or as a holy person or seer, a reliable connection between this psychopathology and religiousness is not scientifically supported.[125]

Personality Disorders

Much as personalities are enduring traits that characterize an individual, personality disorders are enduring behavioral and thought patterns that interfere with normal, successful social functioning. Among these numerous disorders are the self-aggrandizing and strikingly egocentric *narcissistic personality disorder*,[126] the frighteningly unfeeling and potentially dangerous *antisocial personality disorder*, and the withdrawn and fearful *avoidant personality disorder*. *Borderline personality disorder* is characterized, in part, by a distorted self-image and instability in interpersonal relationships, in part because of abandonment concerns.

125 For a more helpful and nuanced treatment of how various psychopathologies, including schizophrenia, can help shed light on religious expression, see McCauley, R. N., and Graham, G. (2020), *Hearing Voices and Other Matters of the Mind: What Mental Abnormalities Can Teach Us about Religion*, Oxford University Press.

126 Though I am not aware that a robust scientific-theological literature exists in this regard (yet), it seems plausible that many models of doing church could provide a space for narcissists to receive inadvertent encouragement in their pathology. Being the primary spiritual, moral, and relationship teacher and leader for hundreds or thousands of people, and being treated as a star on a performance stage, may attract narcissists. But because humility is a prominent Christian value, narcissist pastors may learn that they get more ego-feeding attention if they don't promote themselves as much as surround themselves with other people who admire and promote them, and so are more "covert" in their narcissism. Consider Chuck DeGroat's (2020) *When Narcissism Comes to Church: Healing Your Community from Emotional and Spiritual Abuse*. InterVarsity Press.

Eating Disorders

Sometimes our relationship with even basic needs like food can be deeply disordered. Eating disorders include *anorexia nervosa*, *bulimia nervosa*, and the more common *binge eating disorder*.

Eating Disorders and Augustinian Account of Sin
by Joanna Leidenhag

The influence of Saint Augustine's account of human psychology, particularly with regards to sin, cannot be overstated. And yet, a paradox lies at its heart: how can humans choose a compulsion, and subsequently be compelled to have greater control over their lives? I do not claim to resolve this paradox, but to allow recent work on the psychology of eating disorders to illuminate the discussion. Surely the psychological literature on eating disorders can help us make sense of Augustine's notions of pride and *consuetudo,* and Augustine's multifaceted account of the will can help psychologists make sense of the role of the will within a compulsive disorder.

Leidenhag, J. (2018). Forbidden Fruit: Saint Augustine and the Psychology of Eating Disorders. *New Blackfriars,* 99(1079) (Jan. 2018), 47-65.

Autism Spectrum Disorder (ASD)

This disorder (formerly autism and Asperger's Syndrome) is a developmental disorder characterized by pervasive social and communication challenges. Early signs may include poor eye contact, not following declarative pointing to the degree that is typical, and not wanting normal levels of human contact. These signs have led some theorists to argue that the heart of the disorder is a much weaker than typical ability to understand the mental states of others, perhaps coupled with a much stronger than typical attention to organizing and systemizing features of the environment.[127] Some people suffering from ASD, however, have unusual sensitivity to sensory stimuli such as sounds or touch, which does not easily map onto the "mindblindness" perspective. How to characterize ASD is still debated and developing, but it appears to be increasingly more common in some (but not all) societies.[128]

Autism Spectrum Disorder is attracting the attention of theologians. For instance, Joanna Leidenhag has begun exploring how psychological research into sensory processing differences in adults with ASD can inform new understandings of worship. She suggests that sensory differences, such as hyper- or hypo-sensitivities highlight how the presence of God can be experienced differently through the material world around us. Intentionally neurodiverse

127 For instance, a brief and intriguing but now dated argument along these lines was developed by Simon Baron-Cohen (*Mindblindness: An Essay on Autism and Theory of Mind*, 1997, MIT Press). Though the consensus around ASD has changed since Baron-Cohen's work in the 1990s, his autism-inspired observations concerning the operations of the human theory of mind or "mentalizing" system remain important.

128 McCauley and Graham (2020), include a helpful chapter on ASD in relation to religious thought and expression.

worship may also illuminate one way that justice is practically essential for the church's true worship.[129]

Trauma

Commonly the etiology of psychological disorders include trauma of one sort or another. A trauma is an emotionally disturbing, deeply distressing event, one that challenges, stretches, or even overwhelms one's coping strategies. Notice that such a definition of *trauma* places the emphasis on what an event does to a person's psyche and how an event is emotionally and cognitively processed. And so, though some kinds of events such as the violent death of a loved one or being subject to physical abuse are more likely to be traumas for individuals, an event is not a trauma intrinsically. Stressful and trying events happen to all of us. It seems likely, then, that a lot of human suffering could be avoided if we all had better tools for reducing the ability of an event to traumatize, or if we had better coping skills for reducing the traumatic impact of an event. Coping, resilience, and treatment in the face of trauma, then, are common concerns for scientists and mental health professionals working in this space.[130]

It has not escaped the notice of theologians, especially

129 Leidenhag, J. (2021). Autism, Doxology, and the Nature of Christian Worship,' *Journal of Disability & Religion* (forthcoming online in about a week). I thank Joanna for helping me summarize her work on this topic. Also consider Grant Macaskill's, *Autism and the Church: Bible, Theology, and Community* (2019, Baylor University Press), and Joanna Leidenhag's (2021), "Accountability, Autism, and Friendship with God," *Studies in Christian Ethics*, 1-15, doi: 10.1177/09539468211009759. https://research-repository.st-andrews.ac.uk/bitstream/handle/10023/23014/Leidenhag_2021_SCE_Autism_CC.pdf. See, too: https://www.theo-puzzles.ac.uk/2021/02/23/jleidenhag/

130 One of the field leaders in the psychology of religion and coping is Kenneth Pargament. Many of his contributions are curated here. https://www.kennethpargament.com/key-papers.

those concerned with pastoral issues and ecclesiology, that the church has the ability to be a community that reduces or increases trauma, that provides either beneficial or harmful resources for coping. There is also a growing recognition that the demands of some roles in the church expose these ministers to the risk of being traumatized. How, then, can ministry leaders be better equipped to be resilient in the face of challenging events, to cope with trauma, and to help reduce the trauma in those they serve?[131]

Theologian Erin Kidd observes that there is growing theological engagement with the psych science of trauma:

Theological Engagement with Trauma by Erin Kidd

There is a growing theological engagement with the psych science of trauma. For example, in *God and the Victim*, Jennifer Beste engages with research on the developmental effects of severe and long-term child abuse.[132] Many children in these situations never develop the capacity to relate to themselves, others, or God in a healthy way. For Beste this research calls into question the universality and efficacy of God's love and the human capacity to

131 Preston Hill, for instance, has been very concerned with theologically engaging the scientific study of trauma: https://www.youtube.com/watch?v=qi8e3jPw4h4. Scott Harrower is a psych science-engaged theologian working on similar topics: https://www.ridley.edu.au/resource/trauma-and-christian-recovery/. Psychologists engaged in trauma-related research relevant to Christian spirituality and the church include my former colleagues Joseph Currier, Cynthia Eriksson, Candace Coppinger Pickett, and Lisseth Rojas-Flores. Consider, for instance, this discussion by Eriksson concering the book of Lamentations: https://www.youtube.com/watch?v=T2pW9G-4dU1E.

132 Jennifer Beste, *God and the Victim: Traumatic Intrusions on Grace and Freedom* (Oxford University Press, 2007).

respond to God's grace. It demands an articulation of both grace and freedom that can respond to severe interpersonal harm these children face. Beste argues the answer lies in an understanding of grace as mediated socially—just as we are capable of severely harming and being harmed by each other, so also are healthy communities that prevent and respond to abuse mediations of God's love in this world. See also Cynthia Hess whose engagement with trauma leads her to push the Christian non-violence tradition further, arguing that peace churches must not stop at protesting or refraining from violence but being active in building healthy communities.[133] And Julia Feder engages with psych science and evolutionary anthropology in her work on trauma, wisdom, and suffering—arguing that our vulnerability to harm and our religiosity depend on human capacities that share an evolutionary history.[134]

Psychological Treatment

Though the professional practice of treating psychological

133 Cynthia Hess, *Sites of Violence, Sites of Grace: Christian Nonviolence and the Traumatized Self* (Lanham: Lexington Books, 2009)

134 Julia Feder, "Human suffering, Evolution, and Ecological Niches: Edward Schillebeeckx in Dialogue with Niche Construction Theory," *Journal of Religion & Society* Supplement 16 (2019): 150–64; "Traumatic Violence and Christian Wisdom: Possibilities for Wounding and Healing," in *Evolution of Wisdom: Major and Minor Keys*, ed. Augustín Fuentes and Celia Deane-Drummond (Notre Dame, Ind.: Center for Theology, Science, and Human Flourishing, 2018): 160–69; "Edward Schillebeeckx and Sexual Trauma: Salvation as Healing," *Salvation in the World: The Crossroads of Public Theology*, ed. Stephan van Erp, Christiane Alpers, and Christopher Cimorelli (New York: Bloomsbury, 2017); "The Impossible is Made Possible: Edward Schillebeeckx, Symbolic Imagination, and Eschatological Faith," *Philosophy, Theology, and the Sciences* Special Issue on The Evolution of Wisdom 3:2 (2016): 188–216.

disorders falls outside of "psychological science" as presented here, the evaluation of treatment techniques and interventions is an ongoing application of psychological science. Even if I were to draw upon the available scientific literature, arguing for the superiority of one particular therapeutic orientation would be a bit like arguing for the superiority of Orthodox over Roman Catholic Christianity, or Reformed theology over Wesleyan: likely to raise many objections and caveats and unlikely to persuade anyone who isn't on the 'winning side.' Evidence can be marshalled for the effectiveness of most mainstream treatments for at least some conditions.[135] And so, if I were wanting to use scientific evidence to adjudicate among various possible treatments, I would get specific and look for evidence that helps me answer:

- Is a specific type of psychotherapy or treatment more effective for this specific condition?
- Might a combination (e.g., talk therapy plus medication) be more effective than any one alone?
- Would a particular individual patient/client be more responsive to a specific treatment (e.g., because of their personality, expectations, life demands, etc.)?
- What are possible unintended consequences of a given course of treatment?

Importantly, I would more heavily emphasize evidence generated by studies that have used appropriate control conditions, ideally true clinical experimental studies.

135 With thanks to Mark McMinn, for a listing of some meta-analyses and reviews providing evidence see: https://kspope.com/hospices/meta-analyses.php

Just as someone could be an excellent chef with misguided understandings of food chemistry, someone can be an effective psychotherapist with misguided views of basic psychological dynamics. Sometimes techniques just work, even if the reasons they work are hidden or misunderstood. Nevertheless, all else being equal, I would trust a psychological treatment strategy that is based upon our best understanding of how minds develop and work in relation to their environments.

Opportunities for Theological Engagement

The greatest degree of theological engagement with any area of psychological science concerns psychological health, disorders, pathology, and treatment. Primarily these efforts focus on how theology can inspire and inform mental health research and practice.[136] In principle these integrative efforts could run in the other direction. How might the psychological sciences that concern mental health spur new theological reflection? For instance, Elizabeth Antus argues that theologians might deepen their understanding of the doctrine of the communion of the saints by recognizing the suffering of suicidal people and destigmatize suicide. [137] Jessica Coblentz engages with psychological science in her theological work on depression, and also argues that the psychological sciences could benefit by learning from

---

136 A helpful review of such approaches is William Hathaway and Mark Yarhouse's *The Integration of Psychology and Christianity: A Domain-Based Approach* (IVP Academic, 2021). Also consider Mark McMinn's Sin and Grace in Christian Counseling: An Integrative Paradigm (InterVarsity, 2008).

137 Antus, E. (2020). 'The Silence of the Dead': Remembering Suicide Victims and Reimagining the Communion of Saints. *Theological Studies* 81, 394–413.

theological debates about human suffering.[138] In her work on trauma, Erin Kidd engages with psych science to urge churches to distinguish maladaptive coping mechanisms from sinful behavior; mistaking the former for the latter often causes additional harm to those who suffer trauma, a fact that is particularly pernicious when their trauma is a result of abuse within the church community.[139]

138 Coblentz, J. (2020). What Can Theology Offer Psychology? Some Considerations in the Context of Depression. *Journal of Moral Theology* 9(1), 2–19. This was in a special issue of theology and psychology, the rest of which may also prove helpful.

139 Kidd, E. (2019). The Violation of God in the Body of the World: A Rahnerian Response to Trauma. *Modern Theology* 35(4), 663–82. I thank Erin Kidd for much of the material in this paragraph.

FOUR
Other Specialties

So far I have been providing overviews of the kinds of concentrations that would earn a chapter in an introductory text in psychology and have been common stand-alone courses for many psychology degrees. But as I indicated at the outset, psych science is not coextensive with psychology. Furthermore, there are scientific research areas that are very psychological in character and which borrow elements from other disciplines or cut across traditional psychology sub-fields. In what follows I sketch the general contours of some of these less familiar spaces that I suspect would be interesting for many theologians.

Positive Psychology[140] & Positive Youth Development

Positive psychology and positive youth development have

140 A website dedicated to positive psychology that curates resources in the area is positivepsychology.com. Another site that curates accessible research and application in these "positive" areas is Greater Good at the University of California at Berkeley: https://greatergood.berkeley.edu.

numerous similarities that lead them to be commonly mistaken for each other, but their origins are importantly different. Though foreshadowed by the humanistic psychology movement of the 1960s,[141] positive psychology emerged in the 1990s and 2000s as a reaction against clinical psychology's focus on human brokenness and social psychology's apparent preoccupation with human failures such as reasoning mistakes, out-group degradation, and aggression. Pioneers of the concentration, such as Martin Seligman and Ed Deiner, wondered whether psychological science could contribute to the promotion of human wellbeing and flourishing; what if psychology was not just about helping people be less miserable?[142] The scientific study of happiness or "subjective well-being,"[143] character strengths and virtues (such as forgiveness, gratitude, self-control, grit, and patience), and other indicators of life going well (such as flow states) have come to characterize positive psychology.

Positive Youth Development (PYD) also stresses the potential of people and their communities to not just be okay but to thrive. Like positive psychology, PYD tries to focus on those factors that would be valuable to promote and not just those factors that need to be avoided to live a flourishing or thriving life.[144] Character strengths, virtues, subjective well-being, and other features of positive psychology have a place here, but PYD's origins are in

141 https://www.britannica.com/science/humanistic-psychology

142 https://www.youtube.com/watch?v=flqx4zjLljI

143 A website with many resources including synopses, references, and applications, is the Pursuit of Happiness: https://www.pursuit-of-happiness.org/

144 A quick synopsis of such an approach is given here by PYD leader, Richard Lerner. https://www.youtube.com/watch?v=V-JDByTeT6I Another major figure in PYD's emergence was Peter Benson. Here is his TEDx talk: https://www.youtube.com/watch?v=TqzUHcW58Us.

developmental psychology, particularly approaches that recognize that in order for individual people to live thriving lives, they must be part of and contribute to families, friendships, and communities—including faith communities—that are also showing signs of thriving.[145] Several psychological researchers have found connections between this notion of a thriving life having reciprocating personal and social dimensions as resonate with Christian theology.[146]

Cultural Psychology & Psychological Anthropology

Doing cross-cultural investigation of a particular area of human thought or behavior can be a valuable way to explore how generalizable findings are. In principle, one could do cross-cultural social, cognitive, developmental, or any other psychology. But in addition to employing cross-cultural research techniques, some psychological scientists fully identify as cultural psychologists. Their interest is not merely in how cultural differences add variability (or not) to otherwise stable psychological effects, but how cultural conditions fundamentally shape the way people think, feel, relate, and act. Some cultural psychologists even want to move beyond conventional psychological models, theories, and research methods, and encourage the development of culture-specific psychologies.

---

145 The PYD movement has a very applied face to it with organizations attempting to move theory to research and into practice such as the Search Institute (https://www.search-institute.org) and the Thrive Center for Human Development at Fuller Seminary (https://thethrivecenter.org).

146 Consider Balswick, J. O., King, P. E., and Reimer, K. S. (2016). *The Reciprocating Self: Human Development in Theological Perspective*. IVPress Academic. Pam King has written and co-written many articles on this topic and she joined me in writing *Thriving with Stone Age Minds: Evolutionary Psychology, Christian Faith, and the Quest for Human Flourishing* (2021, IVPress Academic).

Cultural psychology overlaps considerably with psychological anthropology.[147] The research topics may be the same and even some research methods are comparable. If there is a difference, it is that, in general, psychologists — including cultural psychologists — are more comfortable with quantitative and more standardly "scientific" research methods than are anthropologists, including psychological anthropologists. A psychological anthropologist might, for instance rely more on participant-observation whereas a cultural psychologist would be more likely to conduct field experiments. Tanya Luhrmann's study of Vineyard churches is a fine example of psychological anthropology that, while relying on fairly traditional anthropological observation and interview techniques, is very much informed by psychological science.[148]

Some psychological anthropologists are also interested in the flip-side question that drives most cultural psychologists and other psychological anthropologists. Instead of exploring how thought and behavior is the product of culture, they might wonder what features of human psychology make the emergence of cultures possible. As this is an importantly different research project, this concentration will be addressed in the next section.

---

147 For instance, see https://www.psychologytoday.com/intl/blog/sex-drugs-and-boredom/200909/what-is-psychological-anthropology

148 Luhrmann, T. (2012). *When God talks back: Understanding the American Evangelical Relationship with God*. Knopf. Another interesting example is Brian Malley's psychologically informed study of a baptist church in Ann Arbor, Michigan in *How the Bible Works: An Anthropological Study of Evangelical Biblicism*, (2004, AltaMira).

Cognitive Anthropology[149] & Cultural Evolution[150]

It would not be off the mark to think of *cognitive anthropology* as a specific type of psychological anthropology, one very much focused on reasoning, perception, thinking, language, decision-making, and other areas associate with cognitive psychology and cognitive science. Nevertheless, recent decades have seen a growing emphasis on how to use general features of human psychology, especially cognitive regularities, to account for the emergence, spread, and stability of cultural forms. How does human cognition inform and constrain cultural expression such as shared values, games and sports, food procurement and preparation, language, arts, clothing, ritual, and worship? What is it about human cognition that makes "culture" even possible?

This shift from thinking about "culture" as a cause of cognition to "culture" or elements of "culture" as a consequence of cognition blurs, too, with the emergence of *cultural evolution* as an area of study. Cultural evolution, at least as the moniker is used today, captures at least three related projects. First, it concerns how cognitive capacities and common psychological tendencies provide selective pressure on what kinds of values and activities will likely emerge and stabilize in a population such that they are recognizably cultural. Second, cultural evolution concerns how humans and some other species evolved such that cultural forms become part of their experiences. How did humans become so importantly cultural? Likewise, how do

149 Harvey Whitehouse and Emma Cohen, two contributors to contemporary cognitive anthropology, defend a connection between the cognitive sciences and anthropology focused on cooperation here: https://www.eva.mpg.de/documents/Wiley-Blackwell/Whitehouse_Seeking_TopicsCogScience_2012_1563171.pdf.
150 https://culturalevolutionsociety.org/story/What_is_Cultural_Evolution

the capacities that undergird cultural expression develop in early childhood, such as the ability to attribute thoughts to others, to jointly intend to accomplish a goal with another, to use language, and to categorize things and people in the world in particular ways. Finally, cultural evolution concerns how cultures themselves "evolve" over time. Are there predictable and explicable patterns in how certain cultural forms change, say, in interaction with ecological factors or with the size and complexity of a society? Cultural evolution draws broadly on the sciences to address these questions, including psychological sciences.

Evolutionary & Comparative Psychology

The term *evolutionary psychology* has come to represent both an approach or metatheory and a subfield within psychological science. Increasingly, psych scientists of various stripes (developmental, social, cognitive, etc.) bring evolutionary perspectives into their work. Explanatory depth may be gained by considering how selective pressures of the past may have endowed humans with particular psychological traits that they have now. Such a perspective can generate new hypotheses and help account for otherwise peculiar cross-cultural tendencies in humans such as the already mentioned easily acquired fear of snakes even in places where snakes are not an important danger. Adopting an evolutionary perspective helps generate new testable experiments that can lead to new insights about human thought and behavior.

"Evolutionary psychology" is also a term that is sometimes used to label psych scientists who are primarily interested in how human psychology evolved instead of how it operates in contemporary societies. This work often involves combining evidence of various types including contemporary experiments (in the lab or in the field), computer modeling, ethnographic studies of small-scaled people groups, analysis of material remains, and behavioral genetics.[151]

Even more narrowly, critics of evolutionary psychology often use the term to mean a very particular school of thought associated most prominently with Leda Cosmides and John Tooby, who have championed a view that human minds as we find them today are not only importantly the product of the challenges that faced our Stone-aged ancestors, but that human minds are best understood as collections of instinct-like thought and behavioral routines.[152]

The word "comparative" in comparative psychology refers to comparing different species to better understand a particular phenomenon. Naturally, this technique is especially helpful if one suspects that a particular thought or behavioral tendency is driven by environmental factors that might be shared across species, or if a trait is hypothesized to be the part of inherited endowment from common

---

151 A common misunderstanding concerning evolutionary sciences is that they are not subject to the demand for replication. After all, you can't replicate something that happened in the past. But this objection confuses the production of empirical evidence via replicable studies and the subsequent inferences drawn from that evidence. The situation is similar for many scientific treatments of past events such as those studied by astronomers, forensic scientists, and geologists.

152 A very influential touchstone paper in this area is Leda Cosmides & John Tooby's web-published "Evolutionary Psychology: A Primer." https://www.cep.ucsb.edu/primer.html It is worth noting that Cosmides is a psychologist by training and Tooby is an anthropologist. Why? Because their approach is sometimes unfairly criticized as being culture-blind. Evolutionary psychology is notorious for its research concerning sexual attraction and mating. For a presentation of some of this research by one of evolutionary psychology's leading figures, see this TEDx talk by David Buss: https://www.youtube.com/watch?v=mu4Uki8VyLc.

ancestors. Through comparative psychology, human thought and behavior can be compared with other social animals such as dolphins, orcas, wolves, chimpanzees, or with other great apes. Memory, perception, and communication systems in humans might even be fruitfully studied by comparisons with birds. Learning principles have long been studied in many other animals (rats and pigeons most famously), that have applications in humans. For these reasons, it is not uncommon for departments of psychology at major research universities to have animal labs.

Various Sciences of "Religion"

Psychology of Religion[153]

William James did it. So did Sigmund Freud. Carl Jung, too. Many major figures in early psychology studied religious thought, identification, practices, and experiences. Though many of these early figures employed techniques that wouldn't be regarded as terribly good science by contemporary standards, they were concerned with finding non-supernatural causes for religious thought and action. With a few notable exceptions, psychology of religion mostly faded into the background during the reign of behaviorism, only to resurface in the 1960s and 1970s. The latter decades of the 20th century saw a great deal of attention on how

---

153 For a broad overview of psychology of religion, consider Ray Paloutzian's *Invitation to the Psychology of Religion*, 3rd edition, (2016, Guilford Press). For several decades Paloutzian was editor of the *International Journal for the Psychology of Religion* and is a prominent expert. A go-to text on psychology of religion measures and research methods is *The Psychology of Religion: An Empirical Approach*, 5th edition, by Ralph W. Hood, Jr., Peter C. Hill, and Bernard Spilka (2018, Guilford Press). Hood is a leader in the study of mystical experiences and of snake-handling practices in some Holiness churches. Hill is the former editor of the *Journal of Psychology of Christianity*. Spilka, now deceased, was a pioneer in developing measures in the psychology of religion.

to measure religiosity, representations of gods (i.e., "god concepts" and "god images"), as well as continued interest in religious experiences, perhaps especially of mystical varieties. Being able to index one's degree of religious devotion, commitment, and participation, or the particulars of certain religious beliefs, enabled psychologists of religion to study the impact of religiosity or religious beliefs on many other domains such as health, psychological coping, racism, and generosity. Notice that in these sorts of studies the religious variables are predictors or causes of various outcomes of interest. That is, in contrast to its early roots, most psychology of religion in the past 70 years has been concerned with explaining what "religion" (usually some form of Christianity) does more than what the causes of different forms of religious thought and practice are. A notable exception has been the small but persistent interest of psychologists in mystical experiences.

More recent decades have seen an increase in granular interests in the causes and consequences of religious expression such as prayer,[154] anger at God,[155] and the impact of attachment styles on God concepts and conversion.[156] I suspect that this broadening research is in part a function of greater funding opportunities (e.g., through the Templeton philanthropies) as well as trends in overlapping

154 Spilka, B. and Ladd, K. (2012). *The Psychology of Prayer: A Scientific Approach*. Guilford. Also, consider this interview with Kevin Ladd, who has emerged as a leader in the psychological science of prayer: https://www.religiousstudiesproject.com/podcast/the-psychology-of-prayer-an-interview-with-kevin-ladd/

155 Exline, J. J. (2019). "Anger toward God and Divine Forgiveness," In E. L. Worthington and N. G. Wade (eds.), *Handbook of Forgiveness, 2nd Edition*. Routledge.

156 For a brief introduction see https://en.wikipedia.org/wiki/Attachment_theory_and_psychology_of_religion. As the references for this entry suggest, Pehr Granqvist and Lee Kirkpatrick are two leading researchers in this area.

areas such as cognitive science of religion, evolutionary studies of religion, and neuroscience of religion.

Cognitive Science of Religion

Cognitive science of religion is primarily the invention of anthropologists of religion and religious studies scholars who turned to the psychological sciences for intellectual resources to help them generate causal explanations for various forms of religious expression. A common theme in this area is that "religion" is not helpfully distinguished as a special domain with its own unique causes and consequences. So-called "religious" phenomena don't have their own special brain regions or neural correlates, they aren't unified by solving special human problems, and they aren't caused by some well-demarcated set of experiences. Rather, most of what we think of as "religious" is continuous with other ways of thinking, feeling, acting, associating, organizing, celebrating, experiencing, and meaning-making. For this reason, the scientific study of religious thought and action is helpfully informed by the scientific study of other thought and action that is shared in groups.

Cognitive science of religion (CSR) shares blurry boundaries with psychology of religion and some research counts as instances in both areas. But in general, psychology of religion takes individual human thoughts, feelings, and behaviors to be its primary unit of analysis, whereas, cognitive science of religion is much more focused on why it is that certain thoughts, behaviors, and so on, become distributed and stabilized within a population. Psychology of religion tries to explain religious psychology (its causes and consequences), whereas cognitive science of religion primarily seeks to explain cultural forms by appealing to underlying psychological and other dynamics. CSR has also made much more use of cognitive developmental psychology and evolutionary psychology than most psychology of religion, which has generally been the work of clinical, social, and social-developmental psychologists. (See the discussion on evolutionary studies of religion, below.)[157]

Because many working in the cognitive science of religion have stressed that much religious thought and action springs fairly naturally from ordinary human psychologies operating in ordinary human environments — the "naturalness thesis" — this work has garnered the attention of philosophers interested in whether these accounts of religious beliefs should count for or against the justification or warrant of such beliefs.[158] Even more theologically, is CSR

157 In my introduction to the Oxford University Press *Handbook for Cognitive Science of Religion* (2021), I develop this comparison further. In addition to featuring topical chapters by many field leaders, this volume also has chapters that explicitly compare CSR with neighboring areas such as the chapter by Richard Sosis which considers evolutionary studies of religion, and the one by Uffe Schjødt concerning neuroscience of religion. Barrett, J. L. (Ed.) (2021). *Handbook for Cognitive Science of Religion*, Oxford University Press.

158 Some examples are: Trigg, R., and Barrett, J. L. (eds.) (2014). The Roots of Religion: Exploring the Cognitive Science of Religion. Ashgate. Visala, A. and Barrett, J. L. (2019). In What Sense Might Religion be Natural? In P. Copan and C. Taliaferro (eds.), *The Naturalness of Belief: New Essays on Theism's Rationality*, pp. 67-84. Lexington Books. Barrett, J. L., Leech, D., & Visala, A. (2010). Can Religious Belief Be Explained Away? Reasons and Causes of Religious Belief. In U. Frey (ed.) *Evolution and Religion*, pp. 75-92. Tectum. Schloss, J. P., Barrett, J. L., Murray, M. J. (2010). Looking Past vs. Overlooking Cognitive Evolutionary Accounts of Religion: A Response to N Barrett. *Journal of the American Academy of Religion*, 78(3), 622-628. Schloss, J. & Murray, M. J. (eds.) (2009). *The Believing Primate: Scientific, Philosophical, and Theological Perspectives on the Evolution of Religion*, Oxford University Press. Barrett, J. L., and Church, I. M. (2013). Should CSR Give Atheists Assurance? On Beer-Goggles, BFFs, and Skepticism Regarding Religious Beliefs. *The Monist*, 93(3), 311-324. See also, Myron Penner's presentation at https://www.youtube.com/watch?v=L-wHkqEWs6c

providing scientific evidence that bears on such ideas as the *sensus divinitatis* (could it)?[159]

Implications for cognitive science of religion for Christian theology and practice are underdeveloped but have hinted at questions such as: Do the psychological foundations of religious thought in early childhood hold implications for religious education?[160] Does the documented tension between more reflective and more automatic God concepts bear on devotional practices or theological teaching? For instance, Erin Kidd argues that being aware of our cognitive tendencies to think of God in certain idolatrous ways—for instance as a being "up there"—can help theologians better communicate Christian doctrine.[161] Do CSR-based theories of rituals cast sacraments and liturgical practices in a different light?[162]

Evolutionary Studies of Religion[163]

Another scientific area that has blurred boundaries with psychology of religion and cognitive science of religion is evolutionary studies of religion (ESR). It isn't uncommon

159 Clark, K. J., & Barrett, J. L. (2010). Reformed epistemology and the cognitive science of religion. *Faith & Philosophy*, 27(2), 174-189

160 Barrett, J. L. (2012). Born Believers: The Science of Children's Religious Beliefs. The Free Press.

161 Erin Kidd, "The Embodied Mind and How to Pray with One," *Putting God on the Map: Theology and Conceptual Mapping*, ed. Erin Kidd and Jakob Karl Rinderknecht (Lanham, Md.: Lexington Books/Fortress Academic, 2018): 19–41.

162 Greenway, T. S. and Barrett, J. L. (2017). "Cognitive Science of Religion." In P. Copan, ed., *Dictionary of Christianity and Science*. HarperCollins. Barrett, J. L. (2012). Toward a Cognitive Science of Christianity. In J. Stump and A. Padgett (eds.), *Blackwell Companion to Science and Christianity*, pp. 319-334. Blackwell. Barrett, J. L. (2015). Cognitive Science of Religion and Christian Faith: How may they be brought together? *Perspectives on Science and Christian Faith*. http://www.csca.ca/wp-content/uploads/2015/11/Barrett2015.pdf. And see the chapter by Myron Penner and Laird Edman in my forthcoming edited volume: Barrett, J. L. (Ed.). (in press). The Handbook for Cognitive Science of Religion. Oxford University Press.

163 See the chapter by Richard Sosis in Barrett, J. L. (Ed.), *The Handbook for Cognitive Science of Religion*, Oxford University Press, forthcoming.

for scholars to contribute to two or even all three of these areas. Indeed, the international society that was established as the International Association for the Cognitive Science of Religion in 2006, added "and Evolutionary" to its name and scope in 2020.[164] So, why set evolutionary studies of religion apart?

Evolutionary approaches to the study of religion have shared with CSR a focus on explaining group- or cultural-level patterns- in contrast to the traditional psychology of religion focus on individual-level phenomena. But whereas CSR was primarily developed by comparative religionists and social/cultural anthropologists turning to the cognitive sciences (including evolutionary psychology) for inspiration, ESR was primarily inspired by theories coming out of evolutionary anthropology and behavioral ecology. Scholars operating in this ESR mode have been much more likely to posit that certain cultural commitments and practices that we typically call "religious" are evolutionary adaptations to solve common human problems such as large group cooperation. For instance, drawing upon William Irons' work, Richard Sosis and collaborators have generated evidence that engaging in rites, ceremonies, and rituals that publicly demonstrate devotion to religious entities and values, generates trust and cooperation in groups, and such cooperation often makes groups (and the individuals that constitute them) more successful in addressing fitness challenges. These dynamics have been addressed by a family

164 https://iacesr.com

of theories variously labeled "costly", "hard-to-fake", and "charismatic-signaling theory."[165]

One way to understand the difference in emphasis between ESR and CSR is that in ESR a focal question is the extent to which religious identifications, beliefs, and practices have evolved because they were fitness-enhancing for individuals or groups. That is, did religious thought and behavior emerge because it helped some individuals or groups face the demands of survival and reproduction effectively? In CSR, the primary research strategy is to focus on the extent to which religious identifications, beliefs, and practices have "evolved" because they were well-supported by ordinary human cognitive systems and how those systems bear on cultural transmission, not necessarily on any biological notion of fitness. Nonetheless, these two broad research programs have many potential points of contact, and the two areas are unified in both their focus on cultural level-phenomena and the use of evolutionary sciences to make explanatory progress.

ESR's connections to psychology of religion has grown in the past decade as more social psychologists taking an evolutionary approach have begun generating and testing hypotheses concerning analogous problems

---

165 For instance: Irons, W. (2001). "Religion as a Hard-to-Fake Sign of Commitment." in *Evolution and the Capacity for Commitment*. R. M. Nesse (ed.), pp. 292 - 309. New York: Russell Sage Foundation. Sosis, R. & Alcorta, C. (2003). Signaling, solidarity, and the sacred: The evolution of religious behavior. *Evolutionary Anthropology*, 12, 264-274. Sosis, R. & Bressler, E. R. (2003). Cooperation and commune longevity: A test of the costly signaling theory of religion. *Cross-Cultural Research*, 37, 211-239. Sosis, R. & Ruffle, B. J. (2003). Religious ritual and cooperation: Testing for a relationship on Israeli religious and secular kibbutzim. *Current Anthropology*, 44, 713-722. Shaver, J. H., Fraser, G. & Bulbulia, J. (2017). Charismatic Signaling: How religion stabilizes cooperation and entrenches inequality, In J. Liddle and T. Shackelford (eds.), *The Oxford Handbook of Evolutionary Psychology and Religion*. Oxford University Press.

on the individual level of analysis. For instance, do individuals who are reminded of religious values behave more pro-socially toward in-group members? If so, then this is evidence consistent with the idea that religious beliefs and values can serve as social-glue, and may have evolved for just this reason.[166]

Neuroscience of Religion[167]

Whereas the group/cultural-level focus of cognitive science of religion and evolutionary studies of religion make them kindred pursuits, neuroscience of religion is more like traditional psychology of religion in its individual (or even sub-individual) level of analysis. Neuroscience of religion attempts to account for religious thoughts, feelings, and especially experiences by appealing to underlying biological structures and processes of the brain. Why did one person have a particular type of mystical experience when another in the same group did not? Could it have been due to unusual temporal lobe activity? Why are some people prone to feelings of divine presence more than others? What are the consequences of prolonged meditation on brain function?

Sometimes these sorts of neuroscientific investigations

---

166 For instance, see the work reviewed by Ara Norenzayan — much by Norenzayan and his collaborators such as Azim Shariff and William Gervais — in his book Big Gods (2013, Princeton University Press). For a more decidedly cognitive approach that still has strong evolutionary themes, consider Jesse Bering's *The Belief Instinct* (2011, Norton). The comparison of these two books is instructive given that both are written by non-theistic experimental psychologists with evolutionary approaches, but Norenzayan's emphasis is more social psychological and Bering's is more cognitive developmental.

167 For a brief review of neuroscience of religion in comparison with cognitive science of religion, consider Uffe Schjødt's chapter in Barrett, J. L. (ed.). (in press). The Oxford Handbook of Cognitive Science of Religion. Oxford University Press. For a more thorough treatment, see Patrick McNamara's The Neuroscience of Religious Experience (2009, Cambridge University Press). McNamara is one of the most accomplished scholars in this area. See also, V. Gay (ed.) (2009). Neuroscience and Religion: Brain, Mind, Self, and Soul. Lexington Books.

are inspired by brain abnormalities and pathology as in the study of so-called near-death experiences (e.g., in cardiac patients, when the brain is deprived of oxygen) or epileptic episodes.[168] But neuroscientific research can also concern much more ordinary neural dynamics associated with religious practices and experiences, such as those operative during prayer or worship.[169]

One of the big takeaways from neuroscience of religion to date parallels the consensus in CSR: as there is no one cognitive mechanism that gives rise to "religion," there does not appear to be any specifically religious brain region, activation pattern, or other neural event that holds the key to religious thought and experience. Different kinds of religious thoughts, practices, and experiences have differing neural correlates, and all of them involve many neural structures. Likewise, efforts to pathologize "religion" by linking it to some brain abnormality has not been successful.

A contribution that neuroscience of religion may be able to make to theological reflection is in providing evidence concerning whether practices or experiences that are thought to be similar from a theological or analytic perspective turn out to be not all that similar in terms of their biological substrates. For instance, from a theological perspective, one might think that corporate, liturgical prayers of confession are importantly similar to unscripted, individual prayers of confession. But perhaps in terms of the activated neural

168 The University of Otago hosted a conference on "Science and the Afterlife" in 2019. Psychological scientists Jesse Bering and Jamin Halberstadt convened the event. Videos from the conference can be found here: https://www.youtube.com/channel/UCbnpMDWkKipU7iBlfdDJn-A

169 For instance, see Ritchie, S.L. (2021). Integrated physicality and the absence of God: Spiritual technologies in theological context. *Modern Theology*. https://doi.org/10.1111/moth.12684

systems, it could be that these two are importantly different and, hence, may have very different consequences.[170]

170 I offer this possibility only as a hypothetical, but it is inspired by research demonstrating that unscripted prayer marshals brain systems similar to those used in talking to another person whereas those active during reciting scripted prayers is more like other recitation. Schjoedt, U., Stødkilde-Jørgensen, H., Geertz, A. W., & Roepstorff, A. (2009). Highly religious participants recruit areas of social cognition in personal prayer. *Social Cognitive and Affective Neuroscience*, 4, 199-207. https://doi.org/10.1093/scan/nsn050

FIVE
Concluding Thoughts

With theologians in mind, I have provided some broad outlines of psychological science. My hope is that this introduction will get theologians off to a good start in bringing psych science to bear on theological questions. I am optimistic, but I am not naïve enough to think that using psych science will be easy from here on out. Next, I will address a few of the remaining anticipated challenges.

Methodological Naturalism

Psychological science, like most sciences, operate within a kind of methodological naturalism. That is, for the sake of their inquiry, they assume that the only permitted explanations are naturalistic. The supernatural or spiritual are not typically entertained as part of explanatory or predictive accounts. I suspect this feature of psych science will be easily accommodated most of the time by simply accepting the scientific account as operating on one or more levels of proximate causes or mechanisms. For instance, layers of psychological accounts of how one comes to have a religious experience (neuro-, cognitive, social, etc.) may, from a theological perspective, be taken to be the natural means by which the divine acts upon and within a person. The psych science may be regarded as a partial, incomplete account waiting to be supplemented by the more expansive (but perhaps less detailed) account that theology can offer. Nevertheless, there may be moments in which a particular piece of psych science resists such easy integration. Suppose that in our ancestral past humans really did have to successfully detect the signs of active spirits, ghosts, and ancestors and propitiate them in order to have successful hunts, crops, and fertility. If so, then superhuman beings exercised selective pressure on the cognition and behavior of our ancestors. If this is the case, accounts of the evolution of rituals (e.g., as a mechanism for group cohesion) may have gotten off on the wrong foot and can't simply be integrated into theological perspective. By and large, however, most psych science simply sidelines the activity of supernatural causes as outside their scope rather than requiring a negation of them.

A more serious problem for psych scientists, it seems to me, is when their commitment to methodological naturalism leads them to too quickly dismiss potentially real phenomena as impossible because they are associated with supernaturalism. For instance, Myers and DeWall write, "If ESP is real, we would need to overturn the scientific understanding that we are creatures whose minds are tied to our physical brains and whose perceptual experiences of the world are built of sensations."[171] This viewpoint has led, for instance, to most psychologists dismissing out of hand evidence — including peer reviewed evidence by well-regarded experimental psychologists at reputable institutions — for what are sometimes called psi phenomena. Indeed, if a finding is so disruptive to other well-established findings, then it deserves considerable scrutiny, but does this anti-supernatural worldview interfere with creative and fair appraisal of evidence? Maybe humans really are sensitive to seemingly spooky alternative forms of perception that aren't "extrasensory" but different sensory?[172] After all, other organisms apparently can sense and act upon energy types that humans are not consciously aware of. Another example of (perhaps) being too skeptical because of certain naturalistic assumptions is how Myers and DeWall introduce the "empirical approach" of psych science by relaying James Randi's alleged debunking of "those who claim to see glowing auras around people's bodies."[173] Randi (and apparently Myers and DeWall) thinks that someone who claims to see auras can be demonstrated to be a fraud if the aura seer cannot determine the location of a person behind a wall barely taller than the person. Clever, right? But suppose that isn't how auras work. It could be that some people really do see auras, in much the same way that some people really do perceive sounds as having colors:

171 Myers & DeWall, 2018, p. 257.

172 See Myers & DeWall, pp. 257-259, and especially the work cited and other works by Daryl Bem as examples. I once saw Bem present his research findings to a very skeptical audience. He denied that he thought anything "supernatural" was going on, only that psych scientists had adopted a narrow view of what was possible in a naturalistic worldview.

173 Myers & DeWall, p. 2.

they experience synesthesia, a real and well-documented set of phenomena.[174] If so, the aura is a post-perception sensory add-on of the synesthete's and not some glow radiating out of a person even when unperceived. Randi's test makes hidden assumptions based upon his *a priori* views about what is possible. My point here is not to defend spooky parapsychological phenomena. I have no dog in this fight. My point is that, in some cases, the assumptions that psych scientists bring to their studies limit the kinds of explanations that they are willing to entertain, and so they may discard some possibilities toward which some theological approaches may be more hospitable.[175]

Not So Scary Reductionism

It is common practice in psychological science to "reduce" complex phenomena into constituent parts. The motivation for such a research strategy springs from sharing many of the methodological assumptions of the natural sciences. If we want to understand how a complex system works, it can be helpful to break it down into subsystems and those down into constituent parts. We figure out the properties of the parts, and then how they work in subsystems, and then how those subsystems contribute to the system. In this

---

174 For a fascinating, accessible, and efficient introduction to synesthesia, see Ward, J. (2008), *The Frog who Croaked Blue: Synesthesia and the Mixing of the Senses*, Routledge.

175 I am also leaving aside the question as to whether a theist or pantheist should adopt methodological naturalism. For a discussion about methodological naturalism in the sciences and implications for theological engagement, see these articles by Andrew Torrance and John Perry and Sarah Lane Ritchie: Torrance, A. B. (2018). The possibility of a theology-engaged science: a response to Perry and Ritchie. Zygon, 53(4), 1094- 1105. https://doi.org/10.1111/zygo.12475. Perry, J. & Ritchie, S. L. (2018). Magnets, magic, and other anomalies: In defense of methodological naturalism. *Zygon: Journal of Religion & Science*, 53(4), 1064-1093. https://doi.org/10.1111/zygo.12473

sense, then, psychological scientists are (often) unapologetic reductionists. But when theologians or other humanities scholars accuse scientists of being "reductionists," I take it that they mean something more sinister: that the scientists are trying to eliminate or explain away a particular level of being. The worry, if I understand it correctly, is that human thought, feelings, sociality, virtues, and so on, will be (mistakenly) regarded by the scientist as nothing more than what they can study in the lab. The whole is not greater than the sum of its parts.

Scientists of various stripes have probably rightly earned the reputation of sometimes too quickly taking their reductive methodology to warrant ontological reduction or eliminativism.[176] Scientists can sometimes be like the carpenter who is so good with a hammer that everything starts looking like a nail. It doesn't follow, however, that nothing is a nail. That is, sometimes, it is very useful to reduce what looks very complex into constituent parts and to be open to discovering how the parts contribute to the whole. And maybe some of those parts are more important than others. If my bicycle doesn't work because my chain is broken, I want the chain fixed not a new paint job or a whole new bike. Many times, reduction works rather well.

But in my experience, most good psychological scientists do not forget the whole. Psychological scientists go into this field because they are fascinated by people, their thoughts, motivations, and behaviors. It does not escape their attention that human lives are complex wholes, situated in complex social and cultural systems. And their

176 Though as Michael Burdett suggested to me, journalistic and other popular treatments of the sciences may bear some responsibility in this regard.

training has taught them that their measures and protocols are merely methods to roughly and indirectly get an explanatory handle on something much more complex than can be fully studied in the lab. Most psychological scientists are fully aware that when they make a discovery, they often have only "explained" a tiny fraction of the phenomenon under consideration. (One of the reasons that scientists can be such poor communicators of their research to the unindoctrinated is because of the nature of their training, which requires nuance, caveat, and sometimes the specificity of terms that carry meaning within, but not outside, the community.) Indeed, currently most reputable psychological science journals require that researchers report "effect sizes" from their studies. Even after narrowing the phenomena under consideration, psychological scientists are happy with a finding that "explains" 20% of the variance in a dataset (let alone the data not collected!) They know that they have only a partial grasp on the problem they want to understand better. Their goal is to grow that little bit of understanding; to see how the little parts form bigger systems. Indeed, I don't know that psychological scientists are any more "reductionistic" (in the negative sense) than medical doctors, but we don't commonly refuse the advice of physicians on the basis that they are reductionists.

And so, it is perhaps short-sighted for theologians to be too quick to accuse psychologists of "reductionism" and indeed counter-productive if that accusation is used as grounds to ignore what psychological scientists have learned. I have witnessed similar dismissiveness because psychological constructs are (allegedly) "thin" instead of "thick," but the metaphorical girth of a construct or explanation must be relevant to the problem at hand if such accusations aren't merely acts of intellectual body-shaming. Even if the psychological construct needs further development, does it provide some useful explanatory purchase? If so, how can it be part of a broader explanation?

My advice for theologians is to give the psychological science (and scientists) the benefit of the doubt before dismissing a certain body of work as being too thin or reductionistic to be of any use. You could be right. Psychological science is young and full of gaps after all. But maybe these craftspeople know when a hammer isn't the right tool, and even if they don't, your building site may have some nails needing pounded.

Operationalization and Decoding Terms

A related challenge for a theologian to make proper use of psychological science is how to translate the key concepts or constructs from psychological science into a form that is useful to the theological project. Psychological scientists sometimes create strange neologisms but also often use terms borrowed from ordinary discourse or from philosophical or even theological treatments of human experiences. Often this appropriation is deliberate and done mindful of the fact that what is actually being studied by them is slightly or even massively different than what a particular author or school of thought meant by the term. It is not a common concern of psychological scientist to try to preserve the carefully nuanced concept that this or that thinker developed when the psych scientist starts their work. They treat the philosopher, theologian, or literary figure as someone who has made an intriguing observation or posed a promising hypothesis. But they do not take the fact that Augustine, Thomas Aquinas, or Karl Barth argued for a particular point as compelling evidence for that point, and they (generally) are not concerned with vindicating the claims of this or that great thinker, even if the thinker is a psych scientist.

In order to communicate their research, psych scientists commonly light upon a common word that comes closest to the phenomenon under scrutiny. That a language has a word for a given concept, feeling, experience, or virtue is only taken as suggestive that there is a psychological kind that reliably maps onto that word. It may be that the actual features of an experience or the dynamics of a feeling are different than what has been captured by language. The result is that a psychological concept may end up looking very different than common usage of its label. For instance, an increasingly common example is how psych scientists use the term 'bias' to mean a processing or associative predilection. If we are inclined to associate bananas with monkeys, we have a bias to group bananas with monkeys. Of course, that use of 'bias' carries none of the negative connotations that the word has in ordinary contemporary discourse.

A consequence of these observations is that there lurks an ever-present danger in assuming erroneously that a psych science finding or theory has a sufficiently strong mapping with a familiar common concept or a theological or philosophical concept because of similar language. The psych science is bringing its own meanings, assumptions, and base of evidence. How, then, can the psych science be productively used without accidentally importing incompatible conceptual baggage?

The strategy that psych scientists use in trying to understand each other is to look closely at how a concept has been operationalized, what a particular term or concept means for a particular study and how it is measured. A psych scientist may claim to be studying, say, cooperation, but inspection of the research methods reveals that "cooperation" is indexed by how much money a person puts into a common pool in an economic game. The psych scientist may or may not offer much by way of argument for why this operationalization of cooperation is appropriate. It is up to the reader to decide whether this narrowed sense of "cooperation" is relevant to the reader's concerns. Commonly, the author and the reader agree that however a concept has been operationalized is narrower than the hoped-for real-world application. But there is usually a tradeoff between being able to reliably and repeatedly measure a particular behavior (its *internal validity*) and its generalizability out of the lab (*external validity*).[177]

The virtue of using a much narrower sense of a concept for the actual study, is that even if one does not accept the theoretical framework or many of the motivations of the study, you may still see how the findings bear upon the kind of human thought or behavior of interest. You may, for instance, discover that a scale that measures "religiosity"

177 This negotiated tradeoff is one of many reasons why we must be cautious in drawing broad conclusions from a single study. Several studies with slightly different operationalizations of the same variable or construct may collectively provide a broader range of both internal and external validity. These conceptual replications (as they are often called) can build a stronger cumulative case.

does not map onto what you mean by *religiosity*, but it does reasonably measure the frequency with which someone engages in collective religious activities, and that is helpful information. And so, unlike many theological or philosophical systems in which rejection of the theoretical framework leaves most of the particulars unhelpful, in psychological science, one need not accept the theoretical framework in order to accept the usefulness of the findings.[178] Indeed, one of the reasons that psychological science has successfully made progress on many fronts is that even when an old theory or framework is discarded, the results that it generated often remain relevant evidence. Behaviorism as a broad framework is no longer positively regarded but the experimental results generated by B.F. Skinner still hold. Cognitive developmentalists think that child development is more gradual and less stage-like than Piaget thought, but many of Piaget's findings can be replicated today and must be accounted for whether you like his theoretical assumptions or not. And so, more important than understanding the theories or assumptions behind how a study was conducted, or its place in the discipline's history, is looking carefully at how the key concepts have been operationalized and what the findings are.

Unfortunately, some terms common in psych science are not operationalized because they are insider jargon that must simply be learned in time. Also unfortunately, some of the words used are the same as used in theology but carrying different meanings. In the section "Some Key Terms, Concepts, and Values," I discussed what a *theory*

178 I take it that this difference has much to do with psych science being strongly abductive in its approach and philosophy and theology being much more deductive.

is for psych scientists. Another troublesome example is *normative*. In psych science the word *normative* is typically used to mean that which is statistically typical, as in, "It is normative for people to hold seven chunks of information in working memory," or "It is normative for a nine-month-old to begin using declarative pointing." These statements do not carry the usual moral, ought-ness that the word carries in theology.[179]

In Conclusion

The scope of psych science is constantly growing and so the potential points of contact with theology are constantly expanding. I can imagine theologians finding this fact exciting but also daunting. Is it possible to keep up with the science sufficiently to make good use of it in theological inquiry? Let me assure you, it isn't. Fortunately, you don't need to.

Returning to my opening metaphor, as the leader of an intellectual building project, you do not need to know all of the possible ways that each of the specialists on your team might contribute. You only need to know the general ways in which they might contribute and when it is those would be valuable contributions. With that general knowledge in hand, you can let the specialists do what they do best. Working with this expertise you can solve specific problems that, perhaps, you couldn't have solved otherwise.

Hopefully this primer has provided you enough of a

179 Notice, however, that there is frequently a subtle 'ought' in many of these psychological claims. Often the psych scientist is saying something about the proper function of some piece of human psychology: if one's working memory is functioning properly for a human being, then it will hold approximately seven chunks of information.

general introduction to give you a sense of when psych science could be helpful to your theological inquiry. You can more confidently determine whether or not a specialist in stonework will add beauty and value to your building. Perhaps you even have stronger and more reliable judgments concerning whether you need a specialist in sandstone versus marble or granite.

I have only given you a broad overview and a sampling of findings and theories but if you ask yourself whether your project has one of the four features I sketched in Chapter 1, you'll know that it is advantageous to look for some psych science.

- Are you making descriptive psychological claims?
- Are you making normative claims supported by descriptive psychological claims?
- Are you making claims about what effects texts, rituals, and practices have on people (such as their thoughts, feelings, attitudes, and behaviors)?
- Are you constructing an argument that uses intuitions as premises?

I am also hoping that this primer, and especially its various footnotes, citations, and links will give you some first steps for looking at particular topics in psych science in greater detail. You may discover that the existing state of the science supports or challenges theological positions to which you found yourself attracted. I encourage you to let the science help you refine your thinking and not merely serve to confirm what you already hope to reveal.

Excellence will come with practice and drawing upon examples of others who have done likewise. In future revisions of this primer, I hope to add more pointers to exemplary theological scholarship that integrates psychological science. (If you have examples, please draw them to my attention!)

At times in your pursuit of this integration, I fear you will find that the existing science has not matured enough to be helpful. In those cases, perhaps your analysis of the question and the empirical gap can encourage scientific treatment of the topic. One of the reasons I am enthusiastic about theologians engaging psychological science is the potential for psych science to grow as a result. Psychological science and theology have greater potential for progress if they work together.

Afterword

This little electronic book was developed to support the growing number of theologians (including philosophers who work on theological topics) who are turning to psychological and other human sciences to enhance their theological scholarship. I am particularly grateful to the philosophers and theologians in the TheoPsych program, who have joined me and my Blueprint 1543 team on this adventure, and I wrote this with them in mind, thanks to funding from the John Templeton Foundation.

I view this primer as a work in progress. If you have suggestions for improvements or links and citations to add, let me know. I would especially value examples of theological works that make good use of psychological science that could serve as inspiration for others. Don't be shy if you have written such a piece. Send a 100-200 word synopsis of the work, highlighting how the psych science helped, along with a citation to the published work, and we will try to work it in as a note or a box in a future edition with appropriate attribution, of course.

About the Author

JUSTIN L. BARRETT received his B.A. in psychology from Calvin University and his Ph.D. in psychology from Cornell University where he was part of a lab group led by cognitive-developmental psychologists Frank Keil and Elizabeth Spelke. His primary research area is cognitive science of religion and he has conducted and collaborated on psych science studies of god concepts, understandings of mind-body relations, memory for cultural concepts, and intuitions concerning religious rituals, among others. His studies have involved children and adults, and participants from dozens of countries. He has held faculty positions in psychology at Calvin University, Fuller Theological Seminary, and the University of Michigan, and helped found the Institute for Cognitive and Evolutionary Anthropology at the University of Oxford. He has published books, book chapters, and articles bearing upon anthropology, art, literary studies, philosophy, psychology, religious studies, and theology. He is now president of Blueprint 1543.

References

American Psychological Association (2020). *Publication Manual of the American Psychological Association, Seventh Edition*. American Psychological Association.

Antus, E. (2020). 'The Silence of the Dead': Remembering Suicide Victims and Reimagining the Communion of Saints. *Theological Studies* 81, 394–413.

Asch, S. E. (1955). Opinions and social pressure. *Scientific American*, 193, 31-35.

Balswick, J. O., King, P. E., and Reimer, K. S. (2016). *The Reciprocating Self: Human Development in Theological Perspective.* IVPress Academic.

Bandura, A. (2006). Toward a psychology of human agency. *Perspectives on Psychological Science*, 1, 164-180.

Bandura, A., Ross, D. & Ross, S. A. (1961). Transmission of aggression through imitation of aggressive models. *Journal of Abnormal and Social Psychology*, 63, 575-582.

Barrett, J. L. (2011). *Cognitive Science, Religion, and Theology: From Human Minds to Divine Minds.* Templeton Press.

Barrett, J. L. (2012). Born Believers: The Science of Children's Religious Beliefs. The Free Press.

Barrett, J. L. (2012). Toward a Cognitive Science of Christianity. In J. Stump and A. Padgett (eds.), *Blackwell Companion to Science and Christianity,* pp. 319-334. Blackwell.

Barrett, J. L. (2015). Cognitive Science of Religion and Christian Faith: How may they be brought together? *Perspectives on Science and Christian Faith.* http://www.csca.ca/wp-content/uploads/2015/11/Barrett2015.pdf.

Barrett, J. L. (2019). Give up childish ways or receive the Kingdom like a child? In T. Crisp, S. Porter, and G. Ten Elshof (eds.), *Psychology and Spiritual Formation in Dialogue: Moral and Spiritual Change in Christian Perspective*, pp. 254-268. Downers Grove, IL: IVP Academic.

Barrett, J. L. (Ed.) (2021). *Handbook for Cognitive Science of Religion*, Oxford University Press

Barrett, J. L. (2021). "Revelation and cognitive science: An invitation." In B. Mezei, F. Murphy, & K. Oakes (eds.), *Oxford Handbook of Divine Revelation*, pp. 518-536. Oxford University Press.

Barrett, J. L., and Church, I. M. (2013). Should CSR Give Atheists Assurance? On Beer-Goggles, BFFs, and Skepticism Regarding Religious Beliefs. *The Monist, 93(3),* 311-324.

Barrett, J. L. with King, P. E. (2021). *Thriving with Stone-aged Minds*. InterVarsity Academic.

Barrett, J. L., Leech, D., & Visala, A. (2010). Can Religious Belief Be Explained Away? Reasons and Causes of Religious Belief. In U. Frey (ed.) *Evolution and Religion,* pp. 75-92. Tectum.

Barrett, J. L., Richert, R.A., & Driesenga, A. (2001). God's beliefs versus Mom's: The development of natural and non-natural agent concepts. *Child Development*, *72*(1), 50-65.

Barrett, J. L. & VanOrman, B. (1996). The effects of image use in worship on God concepts. *Journal of Psychology and Christianity*, *15*(1), 38-45.

Battro, A. M. (2001). *Half a Brain is Enough: The Story of Nico*. Cambridge University Press.

Bering, J. (2011). *The Belief Instinct: The Psychology of Souls, Destiny, and the Meaning of Life.* Norton.

Bloom, P. (2013). *Just Babies: The Origins of Good and Evil*. Broadway Books.

Brown, W. S. & Strawn, B. D. (2012). *The Physical Nature of the Christian Life: Neuroscience, Psychology, and the Church.* Cambridge University Press.

Chabris, C. and Simons, D. (2011). *The Invisible Gorilla: How Our Intuitions Deceive Us.* Harmony.

Church, I. M., Carlson, R., and Barrett, J. L. (2020). Evil Intuitions? The Problem of Evil, Experimental Philosophy, and the Need for Psychological Research. *Journal of Psychology and Theology.*

Clark. K. J. (2019). *God and the Brain: The Rationality of Belief*. Eerdmans.

Clark, K. J., & Barrett, J. L. (2010). Reformed epistemology and the cognitive science of religion. *Faith & Philosophy*, 27(2), 174-189

Clifton, et al. (2019). Primal world beliefs. *Psychological Assessment*, 31, 82-99. http://dx.doi.org/10.1037/pas0000639

Coblentz, J. (2020). What Can Theology Offer Psychology? Some Considerations in the Context of Depression. *Journal of Moral Theology,* 9(1), 2–19.

Cockayne, J. & Slater, G. (2021). Feasts of Memory: Collective Remembering, Liturgical Time Travel and the Actualisation of the Past. *Modern Theology*, 37, 275-295

Cosmides, L. & Tooby, J. (1997). "Evolutionary Psychology: A Primer." https://www.cep.ucsb.edu/primer.html

Crisp, T. M., Porter, S. L., & Ten Elshof, G. A. (eds.) (2019). *Psychology and Spiritual Formation in Dialogue: Moral and Spiritual Change in Christian Perspective*. Downers Grove, IL: IVP Academic.

Crosby, R. G., Smith, E. I., Gage, J. & Blanchette, L. (2021). Trauma-informed children's ministry: A qualitative descriptive study. *Journal of Child and Adolescent Trauma*. Advance online publication. https://doi.org/10.1007/s40653-020-00334-w.

Darley, J. M., and Batson, C. D. (1973). "From Jerusalem to Jericho": A Study of Situational and Dispositional Variables in Helping Behavior. *Journal of Personality and Social Psychology*, 27, 100-108.

Darley, J. M. & Latané, B. (1968). "Bystander intervention in emergencies: Diffusion of responsibility". *Journal of Personality and Social Psychology*. 8,(4, Pt.1), 377–383. doi:10.1037/h0025589. PMID 5645600.

DeGroat, C. (2020). *When Narcissism Comes to Church: Healing Your Community from Emotional and Spiritual Abuse.* InterVarsity Press.

Emmons, R. A. (2003). *The Psychology of Ultimate Concerns: Motivation and Spirituality in Personality.* Guildford.

Emmons, R. A., Hill, P. C., Barrett, J. L., & Kapic, K. M. (2017). Psychological and theological reflections on grace and its relevance for science and practice. *Psychology of Religion and Spirituality, 9*(3), 276-284. http://dx.doi.org/10.1037/rel0000136

Exline, J. J. (2019). "Anger toward God and Divine Forgiveness," In E. L. Worthington and N. G. Wade (eds.), *Handbook of Forgiveness, 2nd Edition.* Routledge.

Fisher, M., Goddu, M.K., & Keil, F.C. (2015). Searching for explanations: How the Internet inflates estimates of internal knowledge. *Journal of Experimental Psychology. General*. 144: 674-87. PMID 25822461 DOI: 10.1037/xge0000070

Galen, L. (2017). Overlapping Mental Magisteria: Implications of Experimental Psychology for a Theory of Religious Belief as Misattribution. *Method & Theory in the Study of Religion*, 29, 1-47. doi: 10.1163/15700682-12341393.

Garcia, J. & Koelling, R. A. (1966). Relation of cue to consequence in avoidance learning. *Psychonomic Science*, 4, 123-124.

Gay, V. (ed.) (2009). *Neuroscience and Religion: Brain, Mind, Self, and Soul.* Lexington Books.

Gilovich T. (1990). *How We Know What Isn't So: The Fallibility of Human Reason in Everyday Life.* The Free Press.

Gladwell, M. (2007). *Blink:The Power of Thinking without Thinking.* Back Bay Books.

Graham, J., Haidt, J., Koleva, S., Motyl, M., Iyer, R., Wojcik, S. P., Ditto, P. H. (2013). Moral Foundations Theory: The Pragmatic Validity of Moral Pluralism. *Advances in Experimental Social Psychology,* 47, 55-130.

Graham, J., Nosek, B. A., Haidt, J., Iyer, R., Koleva, S., Ditto, P. H., (2011). Mapping the moral domain. *Journal of Personality and Social Psychology*, 101 (2), 366.

Greenway, T. S. and Barrett, J. L. (2017). "Cognitive Science of Religion." In P. Copan, ed., *Dictionary of Christianity and Science*. HarperCollins.

Hall, T. W., & Hall, M. E. L. (2021). *Relational Spirituality: A Psychological-Theological Paradigm for Transformation*. Downer's Grove, IL: IVP Academic.

Hathaway, W. L. and Yarhouse, M. A. (2021). *The Integration of Psychology and Christianity: A Domain-Based Approach*. IVP Academic.

Hayes, A. F. (1994). Age Preferences for Same- and Opposite-Sex Partners. *The Journal of Social Psychology*, 135, 125-133.

Henrich, J. (2019). *The Weirdest People on Earth: How the West Became Psychologically Peculiar and Particularly Prosperous*. Farrar, Straus and Giroux.

Henrich, J., & Broesch, J. (2011). On the nature of cultural transmission networks: evidence from Fijian villages for adaptive learning biases. *Philosophical Transactions of the Royal Society B*, 366, 1139-1148. doi:10.1098/rstb.2010.0323

Henrich, J., & McElreath, R. (2007). Dual inheritance theory: The evolution of human cultural capacities and cultural evolution. In R. Dunbar & L. Barrett (Ed.), *Oxford handbook of evolutionary psychology* (pp. 555-570). Oxford, UK: Oxford University Press.

Hermer-Vasquez, L., Spelke, E. S., & Katsnelson, A. S. (1999). Sources of flexibility in human cognition: dual-task studies of space and language. *Cognitive Psychology*, 39, 3-36.

Hood, R. W., Hill, P. C., & Spilka, B. (2018). *The Psychology of Religion: An Empirical Approach, 5th edition.* Guilford Press.

Hornbeck, R. G., Barrett, J. L. and Kang (Hernandez), M. (eds.) (2017). *Religious Cognition in China: Homo Religiosus and the Dragon*. Springer International.

Irons, W. (2001). "Religion as a Hard-to-Fake Sign of Commitment." in *Evolution and the Capacity for Commitment.* R. M. Nesse (ed.), pp. 292 - 309. New York: Russell Sage Foundation.

James, W. (1902). *The Varieties of Religious Experience: A Study in Human Nature*. New York: Longmans, Green & Co.

Jeeves, M. & Brown, W. S. (2009). *Neuroscience, Psychology, and Religion: Illusions, Delusions, and Realities about Human Nature*. Templeton Press.

Kahneman, D. (2013). *Thinking, Fast and Slow*. Farrar, Straus and Giroux.

Kidd, E. (2019). The Violation of God in the Body of the World: A Rahnerian Response to Trauma. *Modern Theology* 35(4), 663–82.

Latané, B. & Darley, J. M. (1968). "Group inhibition of bystander intervention in emergencies". *Journal of Personality and Social Psychology*. 10 (3), 308–324. doi:10.1037/h0026570. PMID 5704479.

Leidenhag, J. (2018). Forbidden Fruit: Saint Augustine and the Psychology of Eating Disorders. *New Blackfriars* Vol. 99(1079): 47-65.

Leidenhag, J. (2021). Accountability, Autism, and Friendship with God. *Studies in Christian Ethics,* 1-15, doi: 10.1177/09539468211009759. https://research-repository.st-andrews.ac.uk/bitstream/handle/10023/23014/Leidenhag_2021_SCE_Autism_CC.pdf

Luhrmann, T. (2012). *When God talks back: Understanding the American Evangelical Relationship with God.* Knopf.

Macaskill, G. (2019). *Autism and the Church: Bible, Theology, and Community.* Baylor University Press.

Malley, B. (2004). *How the Bible Works: An Anthropological Study of Evangelical Biblicism.* AltaMira.

Maslow, A. H. (1971). *The farther reaches of human nature.* New York: Viking Press.

McAdams, D. P. (1995). What Do We Know When We Know a Person? *Journal of Personality*, 63, 365-396. https://www.sesp.northwestern.edu/docs/publications/557464623490a3fc35faeb.pdf

McCauley, R. N., & Graham, G. (2020), *Hearing Voices and Other Matters of the Mind: What Mental Abnormalities Can Teach Us about Religion,* Oxford University Press.

McGrath, A. (2008). *The Open Secret: A New Secret for Natural Theology.* Blackwell.

McGrath, A. (2018). *Christian Theology: An Introduction, Sixth Edition.* Wiley Blackwell.

McKay, R. & Whitehouse, H. (2014). Religion and Morality, *Psychology Bulletin*. http://dx.doi.org/10.1037/a0038455

McMinn, M. R. (2008). *Sin and Grace in Christian Counseling: An Integrative Paradigm.* InterVarsity Press.

McNamara, P. (2009). *The Neuroscience of Religious Experience.* Cambridge University Press.

Milgram, S. (1963). Behavioral study of obedience. *Journal of Abnormal & Social Psychology*, 72, 207-217.

Miller, C. B. (2021). *Moral Psychology*. Cambridge University Press.

Miller, C. B. (2021). *Honesty: The Philosophy and Psychology of a Neglected Virtue.* Oxford University Press.

Murphy, N. & Brown, W. S. (2007). *Did My Neurons Make Me Do It? Philosophical and Neurobiological Perspectives on Moral Responsibility and Free Will.* Oxford University Press.

Myers, D. G. & DeWall, C. N. (2018). *Psychology, 12th edition*. Worth Publishers.

Myers, D. G. & DeWall, C. N. (2021). *Psychology, 13th edition*. Worth Publishers.

Norenzayan, A. (2013). *Big Gods: How Religion Transformed Cooperation and Conflict*. Princeton University Press.

Norrman, G. & Bylund, E. (2016). The irreversibility of sensitive period effects in language development: evidence from second language acquisition in international adoptees. *Developmental Science*, 19, 513-520. doi: 10.1111/desc/12332

Öhman, A., & Mineka, S. (2001). Fears, phobias, and preparedness: Toward an evolved module of fear and fear learning. *Psychological Review,* 108(3), 483-522. https://doi.org/10.1037/0033-295X.108.3.483

Packer, J. I. (1973). *Knowing God.* InterVarsity Press.

Paloutzian, R. (2016). *Invitation to the Psychology of Religion, 3rd edition.* Guilford Press.

Perry, J. & Ritchie, S. L. (2018). Magnets, magic, and other anomalies: In defense of methodological naturalism. *Zygon: Journal of Religion & Science*, 53(4), 1064-1093. https://doi.org/10.1111/zygo.12473

Peterson, G. R. (2002). *Minding God: Theology and the Cognitive Sciences*. Fortress Press.

Purzycki et al. (2018). The cognitive and cultural foundations of moral behavior. *Evolution and Human Behavior*. doi: 10.1016/j.evolhumbehav.2018.04.004.

Ritchie, S.L. (2021). Integrated physicality and the absence of God: Spiritual technologies in theological context. *Modern Theology*. https://doi.org/10.1111/moth.12684

Schloss, J. P., Barrett, J. L., Murray, M. J. (2010). Looking Past vs. Overlooking Cognitive Evolutionary Accounts of Religion: A Response to N Barrett. *Journal of the American Academy of Religion, 78(3),* 622-628.

Schloss, J. & Murray, M. J. (eds.) (2009). T*he Believing Primate: Scientific, Philosophical, and Theological Perspectives on the Evolution of Religion*, Oxford University Press.

Schjoedt, U., Stødkilde-Jørgensen, H., Geertz, A. W., & Roepstorff, A. (2009). Highly religious participants recruit areas of social cognition in personal prayer. *Social Cognitive and Affective Neuroscience*, 4, 199-207. https://doi.org/10.1093/scan/nsn050

Schnitker, S. A., Porter, T. J., Emmons, R. A., & Barrett, J. L. (2012). Attachment Predicts Adolescent Conversions at Young Life Religious Summer Camps. *International Journal for the Psychology of Religion*, 22, 198-215. doi: 10.1080/10508619.2012.670024

Schnitker, S. A., Ratchford, J. L., Emmons, R. A., & Barrett, J. L. (2019). High goal conflict and low goal meaning are associated with an increased likelihood of subsequent religious transformations in adolescents. *Journal of Research in Personality*, 80, 38-42.

Shaver, J. H., Fraser, G. & Bulbulia, J. (2017). Charismatic Signaling: How religion stabilizes cooperation and entrenches inequality, In J. Liddle and T. Shackelford (eds.), *The Oxford Handbook of Evolutionary Psychology and Religion*. Oxford University Press.

Sosis, R. & Alcorta, C. (2003). Signaling, solidarity, and the sacred: The evolution of religious behavior. *Evolutionary Anthropology*, 12, 264-274.

Sosis, R. & Bressler, E. R. (2003). Cooperation and commune longevity: A test of the costly signaling theory of religion. *Cross-Cultural Research*, 37, 211-239.

Sosis, R. & Ruffle, B. J. (2003). Religious ritual and cooperation: Testing for a relationship on Israeli religious and secular kibbutzim. *Current Anthropology*, 44, 713-722.

Spilka, B. and Ladd, K. (2012). *The Psychology of Prayer: A Scientific Approach*. Guilford.

Swinburne, R. (2008). *Was Jesus God?* Oxford University Press.

Tanton, T. (2021). Accommodating Embodied Thinkers. *Modern Theology*, 37, 316-335. doi: 10.1111/moth.12685

Torrance, A. B. (2018). The possibility of a theology-engaged science: a response to Perry and Ritchie. Zygon, 53(4), 1094-1105. https://doi.org/10.1111/zygo.12475.

Trigg, R., & Barrett, J. L. (eds.) (2014). The Roots of Religion: Exploring the Cognitive Science of Religion. Ashgate.

Visala, A. (2014). *Imago Dei*, Dualism, and Evolution: A Philosophical Defense of the Structural Image of God. *Zygon* (Special Edition on Human Nature as *Imago Dei),* 49:1, 101–120.

Visala, A. & Barrett, J. L. (2019). In What Sense Might Religion be Natural? In P. Copan and C. Taliaferro (eds.), *The Naturalness of Belief: New Essays on Theism's Rationality*, pp. 67-84. Lexington Books.

Vassilis, S. (2002). Religion and the five factors of personality: a meta-analytic review. *Personality & Individual Differences*, 32, 15-25. doi: 10.1016/50191-8869(00)00233-6

Watts, F. (2013). Embodied Cognition and Religion. *Zygon* (Special Edition on Religion and Embodied Cognition) 48:3, 745–758.

Wigger, J. B. (2019). *Invisible Companions: Encounters with Imaginary Friends, God, Ancestors, and Angels*. Stanford University Press.

Zahl, S. (2018). Hiding in Plain Sight: The Lost Doctrine of Sin. *Mockingbird*, Oct. 2, 2018. https://mbird.com/theology/hiding-in-plain-sight-the-lost-doctrine-of-sin/

Zahl, S. (2020). *The Holy Spirit and Christian Experience.* Oxford University Press.

Zahl, S. (2021). Beyond the critique of soteriological individualism: Relationality and social cognition. *Modern Theology*, 37(2), 336-361. DOI:10.1111/moth.12686

www.ingramcontent.com/pod-product-compliance
Ingram Content Group UK Ltd.
Pitfield, Milton Keynes, MK11 3LW, UK
UKHW042019190726
13854UKWH00005B/2362